The Illinois Officer's Legal Source Book

The Peace Officer's Bible
Volume II
Civil Liability – Section 1983

Dale Anderson, Anthony A. Polse, & Stephen Scheller

Acknowledgments
Thanks to my wife, Sandy, for your help, support, encouragement, and patience. And thanks to Jim Volpe and Stephen J. Scheller, attorneys, and, more importantly, friends who edited and virtually co-authored materials. This book would not have gotten done (right) without you.

Finally, thanks so much to Suzanne Fell, who talked me through the many computer problems I encountered and edited and formatted the text and to Savannah Fell who created many of the illustrations.

DISCLAIMER
Nothing in this book is intended as law or legal advice. You must not consider it as such. Law and legal advice must come from your legal advisor. No one associated with the writing of this book is your legal advisor. No attorney-client relationship exists as a result of reading this book. Again, the information in this book is not a substitute for legal advice. Every factual situation is different, and if you need legal advice about a particular case or situation, you must seek that legal advice from a competent attorney before acting. Detrimental reliance on this book may not be claimed.

The Authors
Dale Anderson has been a member of numerous state and federal bar associations, including the United States Supreme Court Bar. He has tried every kind of criminal case from speeding to capital murder, both as a prosecutor and a defense attorney. He served as a named partner in the law firm of LaPaglia and Anderson where he engaged primarily in litigation, both criminal and civil. He has written numerous books and manuals for law enforcement and lawyers primarily related to constitutional criminal procedure. He has lectured extensively on subjects related to criminal law and procedure, including a period when he served as a law professor. As a member of the United States Supreme Court Bar, Mr. Anderson focuses on United States Supreme Court doctrine related to constitutional law within the context of law enforcement.

Anthony A. Polse is an attorney and former police officer. Mr. Polse is a certified Force Science Analyst and instructs law enforcement on constitutional issues relating to search and seizure. Mr. Polse is also a former prosecutor for the Lake County State's Attorney's Office in Illinois, where he served in several different divisions and obtained significant trial experience. Mr. Polse is also licensed to practice in the federal courts in Illinois and Arizona. Mr. Polse's former law practice concentrated on labor and employment issues for law enforcement along with Fourth Amendment training and reviews specifically designed for law enforcement. Mr. Polse focuses on Arizona and Illinois law analysis related to CourtSmart and the legal source books. Mr. Polse is the former police legal advisor for the Mesa, Arizona, police department and currently is a deputy county attorney assigned as a first responder liaison for the Maricopa County Attorney's Office in Phoenix, Arizona.

Stephen Scheller has been a practicing attorney for over 30 years. Prior to his current position as a division chief in a prominent Illinois prosecutor's office, he was the chief of the criminal division and supervised over 100 employees. He has prosecuted capital cases and tried over 100 major felony jury trials. While in private practice, he represented individuals on a variety of cases including workman's compensation, personal injury, and civil disputes. Mr. Scheller has taught hundreds of state and federal law enforcement officers across the state on numerous legal issues including criminal law and evidence, procedural issues, and police liability. He has been an adjunct faculty professor for over ten years teaching college students on a variety of legal topics. He has lectured and taught numerous civic groups and attorneys on legal and liability issues. Mr. Scheller has received numerous awards throughout his career from federal, state, and local law enforcement agencies and civic groups. Mr. Scheller is a contributor and legal advisor for CourtSmart and the legal source books. He concentrates his legal analysis on constitutional law issues involving law enforcement.

Printed in the United States of America

TABLE OF CONTENTS

CIVIL LIABILITY – SECTION 1983

Introduction

Civil suits against officers continue to rise at an alarming exponential rate. For example, Section 1983 was enacted by Congress in 1871. For about the next century only about one or two cases per year were filed under 1983. This year well over 100,000 cases will probably be filed.

Officers are vulnerable to such actions because, when they violate the constitutional rights of a suspect/citizen or even an "illegal," they violate the rights of a person who can sue them.

This book, Volume II, is written in the same order as Volume I as much as possible.

Volume II focuses primarily on an officer's powers to investigate crime within the constrictions of the Fourth, Fifth, Sixth, and Fourteenth Amendments. Virtually every time an officer violates a suspect's constitutional rights, the officer is vulnerable to a lawsuit. So almost every time a case is recited in the previous book (Volume I) where evidence was suppressed, an officer (and/or his/her department) could have been successfully sued for the same conduct.

> *Most of the cases cited in this book are Seventh Circuit cases. The Seventh Circuit is the court that includes Illinois, Wisconsin, and Indiana. Because the circuits "borrow"—and are influenced by—cases from other circuits, many cases in this chapter have been decided by other circuits around the country, particularly the Ninth Circuit.*

I. Title 42 USC Section 1983

Title 42 U.S.C. Section 1983 is a federal statute that allows anyone whose constitutional rights are violated by officers to sue the officers, their departments, and their municipalities or jurisdictions. Almost all of the unconstitutional activity discussed in this book is covered by Section 1983. The words of the statute provide,

> "Every person who, under color of any statute, ordinance, regulation, custom or usage, of any State or Territory, subjects, or causes to be subjected, any citizen of the United States or other person within the jurisdiction thereof to the deprivation of any right, privileges, or immunities secured by the Constitution and laws, shall be liable to the party injured in an action at law, suit in equity or other proper proceeding for redress."

Since Section 1983 itself is just the "vehicle" to provide the protection under the constitution, plaintiffs must base their complaints on a particular constitutional amendment in order to recover.

History and background

After the Civil War, Congress thought that state officers in the South, particularly members of the Klan, were violating the civil rights of the blacks. The laws of the southern states did not provide redress for these blacks.

Congress, therefore, created and passed Section 1983 in 1871, also known as the Ku Klux Klan Act.

The United States Supreme Court has permitted the expansion of the Act to include any police conduct, which Congress could never have envisioned would be considered to be constitutional violations in 1871. Congress was originally concerned with the Klan/Sheriffs dressing up in sheets and hanging blacks by whom the Klan felt threatened. To illustrate how broadly this statute is now being interpreted, the courts are now permitting suits to be brought against training facilities which do not properly teach officers the implications related to constitutional law.

Probably the most important events historically related to Section 1983 are:

MONROE V PAPE, 365 US 167 (1961)
MONROE was the landmark case where the Supreme Court held that officers could be sued for violating a suspect's/citizen's constitutional rights.

SECTION 1988 ENACTED (1976)
This statute enacted by Congress permitted the award of attorney's fees for the party that wins the case.

MONELL V NEW YORK CITY, 436 US 658 (1978)
The United States Supreme Court explained that municipalities can be sued if the plaintiffs can prove that the constitutional violation was the result of policy or long-standing practice.

CITY OF CANTON V HARRIS, 489 US 378 (1989)
The United States Supreme Court explained the circumstances under which a department may be sued for failure to train in the area of constitutional law.

GRAHAM V CONNOR, 490 US 386 (1989)
Officers were put on notice that after this case, all excessive force cases, as constitutional torts would be tried under Fourth Amendment standards.

SAUCIER V KATZ, 121 S Ct 2151 (2001)
This United States Supreme Court case explained that if an officer has been shown to be in violation of the plaintiff's constitutional rights, the next matter to be proved is whether there was clearly established law related to the officer's conduct. If there was none, the officer is granted qualified immunity.

PEARSON V CALLAHAN, 555 US 223 (2009)
After this case, courts were no longer required to determine the unconstitutionality of the officer's conduct, only that there was no case(s) on point that would put the officer(s) on notice as to whether or not the officer's conduct was unconstitutional.

Purpose

"[T]he very purpose of Section 1983 was to interpose the federal courts between the states and the people, as guardians to protect the people from unconstitutional actions under the color of state law, whether that action be executive, legislative, or judicial" [MITCHUM V FOSTER, 407 US 225 (1972)].

Again, just as important for the courts is the rationale that states often provide protection in theory but not in reality. The seminal and most important case for this rationale is MONROE V PAPE:

MONROE V PAPE, 365 US 167 (1961)
Officers entered Monroe's home unconstitutionally. The officers then required the residents to stand naked while officers searched every room. Mr. Monroe was taken to the station and unconstitutionally questioned about a murder.

The United States Supreme Court ruled that Monroe had a cause of action under Section 1983.The Court then stated that one of the main purposes of this statutory remedy was "to provide a federal remedy where the state remedy, though adequate in theory, was not available in practice… It is abundantly clear that one reason the legislation was passed was to afford a federal right in federal courts because, by reason of prejudice, passion, neglect, intolerance or otherwise, state laws might not be enforced and the claims of citizens to the enjoyment of rights privileges and immunities guaranteed by the Fourteenth Amendment might be denied by the state agencies."

Forums

A Section 1983 action may be brought in federal district court or state court.

Color of law

Civil suits brought pursuant to 42 U.S.C. Section 1983 require only two things: first that officers violated a citizen's constitutional rights and second that the officers acted under "color of law" in order to be held liable.

To prove that an officer is acting under color of law, the plaintiff need only prove that the officer is exercising that legal authority which he is granted pursuant to state statute or federal statute, rule or regulation, or municipal ordinance. This has been very broadly construed by the courts for some time.

Hypothetical

An officer enters a bar in civilian clothes. As the bar closes and drinks are being cut off, the officer demands another drink. The female bartender refuses to serve him, so he beats her up. Can the bartender sue under Section 1983?

Officers working as private security police can be held to be working under color of state law. And private persons working under authority of the state can be working under the color of state law. See Payton v Rush Medical Center, 184 F3d 623 (7th Cir, 1999), Doe v City of Chicago (below).

MONROE V PAPE, 365 US 167 (1961)

Officers entered Monroe's home unconstitutionally. The officers then required the residents to stand naked while the officers searched every room. Mr. Monroe was taken to the station and unconstitutionally questioned about a murder.

The defendants asserted that the police had no authority to do what they did, so their acts could not have been done under the color of law. The Federal District Court in Illinois agreed.

The United States Supreme Court ruled that the officers were acting under color of law. Therefore, Monroe did have a cause of action under Section 1983.

Doe v City of Chicago, 39 F Supp2d 1106 (N IL 1999)

Doe was involved in an accident, and her car was impounded at the city impound lot. She went to the impound lot and tried to remove the stereo from the car. The employee at the lot refused to allow her to have the stereo. The police were called to the scene, and Doe was arrested. The employee was a private citizen employed by a private company. He therefore sought summary judgment based on the fact that he could not possibly be operating under color of state law.

The Seventh Circuit Court of Appeals ruled there were four tests in the determination of whether a private citizen is acting under color of state law. If a private citizen meets any one of the tests, he/she is acting under color of state law. Here are the four tests:

- State Compulsion Test: Has the state so implicated itself in the defendant's action that the state has in effect compelled the action?
- Public Function Test: Is the private person engaged in conduct that traditionally is the exclusive prerogative of the state?

- Joint Action Test: Is there a meeting of the minds between the defendant and the state about the conduct that denies the plaintiff a constitutional right?
- Nexus Test: Has the state insinuated itself so far that the private person's actions create interdependence between the state and the defendant?

The Seventh Circuit ruled that the second test is one that a reasonable jury could find that the employee operated under. Therefore, summary judgment was not appropriate.

Gibson v City of Chicago, 701 F Supp 666 (1988)
The Chicago Police Department placed Gibson on medical leave and took away his authority to carry a gun, his identification, his shield, and all of his police power. Gibson shot and killed a victim. The victim's family sued the police department.

The Federal District Court ruled that Gibson was not acting under color of state law. Therefore, the victim's family did not have a cause of action against the department.

Lukse v County of Los Angeles, 286 F3d 906 (1998)
Officers of a sheriff's office were required to carry their weapons at all times. During a five-year period, the department experienced 80 incidents of officers brandishing or discharging weapons off duty. During 15 of those incidents, the officers were drinking. The department knew about these incidents, but did little about them. And the department apparently did not take any steps to ensure that the incidents would not occur in the future.

A sheriff's deputy, Kirsch, drank himself up to a .25 blood alcohol content (BAC) in a bar one night while arguing with a man named Huffman. Kirsch then shot and killed Huffman.

Huffman's estate sued the officer and department under Section 1983. An expert witness for the estate testified that the department did not devote sufficient attention to the unlawful use of firearms by "off-duty" deputies nor had the department dealt with the issue of guns and alcohol.

The federal district court ruled that Kirsch was not acting within the scope of his employment and did not act under color of law. The Ninth Circuit Court of Appeals agreed.

Relationship to the exclusionary rule

There is a somewhat complicated relationship between Section 1983 actions and the suppression hearing of the criminal case. Officers should think about it in this way: If evidence is suppressed based on the exclusionary rule, it is a very small step to successful civil suit under Section 1983, as a court has already ruled that the conduct was unconstitutional. That is why every case in Volume I is as important as those in Volume II in assessing liability. The reason is that many courts have decided not to explain whether or not the officer violated the plaintiff's rights when the courts award qualified immunity. So officers cannot be sure anymore that they may be sued for constitutional violations except when courts state that the conduct of the officers was unconstitutional.

However, the opposite isn't always true. Even if the evidence is ruled admissible, officers may still be successfully sued under Section 1983 for a number of reasons. Most importantly, the federal courts do not have to pay any attention to state court decisions about suppression. For example, the Seventh Circuit Court of Appeals has decided on many occasions that there was a Section 1983 cause of action, even after the state court denied the motion to suppress and admitted the evidence [see e.g. Simpson v Rowan, 73 F3d 134 (1995)]. That can be bad news for officers.

Example: Illinois courts have traditionally held that the smell of burning marijuana was an exigency, so officers did not need to get a warrant prior to entering. The Seventh Circuit recently held that officers can be successfully sued for entering homes under that circumstance without a warrant.

Relationship to departmental rules

Departmental rules may be relevant in certain circumstances [Edwards v Thomas, 31 F Supp 2d 1069 (ND IL 1994)]. This may be the case if the rule is introduced against the officer and if the purpose of the rule is to protect the rights of citizens [Scott v Henrich, 39 F3d 912 (1994)].

However, department rules are usually not relevant to the issue of violation of civil rights, as the only real issue is whether the officer violated the victim's constitutional rights—not, did the officer violate or comply with his/her departmental rules. See Scott v Edinburg, 346 F3d 752 (2003) below.

"[T]he violation of police regulations or even a state law is completely immaterial as to the question of whether a violation of the federal constitution has been established." Thompson v Chicago, 472 F3d 444(2006)

Scott v Edinburg, 346 F3d 752 (2003)
An officer, Edinburg, was off duty and drove his car to a hot dog stand. He parked at a gas station next to the stand. He left his keys in the car. Scott got in the car and started to drive it away. Edinburg told Scott that the car was his and to stop. The car's reverse lights came on, and the car backed up toward Edinburg. Officer Edinburg moved aside and yelled, "Stop! Police!" and drew his revolver. As the car then sped forward, the officer fired shots. Scott drove away at a high rate of speed. The officer followed on foot into the street and fired several more bullets. One of the bullets killed Scott.

The parties agreed that Scott died from one of the "first few shots fired by Officer Edinburg, while he was on the gas station property." The parties also agreed that there were 12 to 14 pedestrians in the gas station parking lot. Two witnesses swore under oath that no one was in the direct path of the car and that no one was forced to move away as the car sped off. Edinburg stated that two people were in the path and that others were running away.

Edinburg's instructor "testified that shooting into a moving vehicle and the use of deadly force against a non-dangerous fleeing felon is a violation of police procedures."

The Seventh Circuit Court of Appeals ruled that summary judgment was properly granted for the defendant officer as Edinburg could show that Scott represented a threat of serious bodily injury to those in his wake as he drove away. The court determined that the issue is not one of violation of department policies but whether Edinburg violated the constitutional rights of Scott. Therefore, whether Edinburg violated departmental rules is usually irrelevant to a Section 1983 action.

In common law causes of action it is much more likely that departmental rules will be relevant.

United States v Brown, ___F3d___ (7th Cir 2017)
Chicago officers received a tip that drugs were being sold out of a certain convenience store. Officer Brown went to the store and beat and kicked the employee for several minutes. The officer wrote his

report stating that the employee reached for a gun, unaware that the entire incident was caught on surveillance video.

Brown was charged by the federal government of violation of the employee's (Fourth Amendment) constitutional rights. Brown offered to introduce at trial an "expert witness" from the Chicago Police Department to explain, frame by frame, the video and why Brown's conduct was consistent with the Chicago Police Department's rules, policy, and regulations.

The Seventh Circuit Court of Appeals ruled that the departmental rules were irrelevant and therefore inadmissible. If the department's rules were admissible, that would mean that the department controlled the Constitution of the United States rather than the other way around.

Brown was convicted, and his conviction was affirmed.

> *It is important for all officers to understand that they are always being videotaped and that they can be indicted for constitutional violations—and convicted—even when they are not sued by the victim.*

Statute of limitations

Suits brought against officers under Section 1983 must generally be initiated within two years of the violation. If, for example, the suit is brought for false arrest, the suit must normally be brought within two years of the arrest [Copus v City of Edgerton, 151 F3d 646 (1998)].

One problem is that, if the suit conflicts with the result in the criminal case, the suit must be dismissed [HECK V HUMPHREY, 512 US 477 (1994)].

Viramontes v Chicago, 840 F3d 423 (2016)

Officers arrested Viramontes for swinging at officers during a Puerto Rican street festival. A trial court judge found the defendant guilty of resisting and aggravated assault.

Viramontes then sued the officers for excessive force under Section 1983.

The federal district court judge gave the jury the following jury instruction:

> "Mr. Viramontes actively swung in the direction of a police officer and missed. After he swung, Mr. Viramontes actively resisted the police officer. Any statements to the contrary by Mr. Viramontes, his lawyers, or the witness must be ignored."

The Seventh Circuit ruled that the district court was correct in ruling that no evidence may be received at trial that goes contrary to the facts in the criminal case.

This does not mean that an officer cannot be found liable of excessive force even if the defendant was found guilty of the crimes charged. Gilbert v Cook, 512 F3d 899 (7th Cir 2008).

But "if success on the defendant's claims would have necessarily implied the invalidity of a potential conviction of the... charge, then the defendant's claims did not accrue until the day on which the charge was dismissed" [Washington v Summerville, 127 F3d 552 (1997)].

Rosado v Gonzalez, 832 F3d 714 (2016)
Gonzalez, a Chicago police officer, pulled over a car driven by Rosado for failing to use a turn signal. After the stop, the officer(s) "claim to have seen" a badge and handcuffs as well as a handgun in plain view "between the brake lever and center console." The officers arrested Rosado for unlawful possession of a weapon by a felon and for violating the armed habitual criminal statute.

Rosado fought the criminal charges in jail for a year and a half, at which time he received a copy of the dashcam video which reflected that Rosado did use his turn signal. The trial court, relying on the video, granted Rosado's motion to quash his arrest and suppressed all evidence discovered after the unconstitutional stop and detention. The state then dismissed the case.

Approximately two and a half years after his arrest, Rosado filed a Section 1983 action claiming false arrest, conspiracy, and failure to intervene arising from the false arrest.

The federal district court ruled that the claims were "indisputable time-barred" by the statute of limitations.

The Seventh Circuit ruled that the "statute of limitations for a false-arrest claim begins to run at the time the claimant becomes detained pursuant to legal process, meaning when the claimant is bound over for trial." Wallace v Kato, 549 US 384 at 391.

Rosado tried to argue that since the video was withheld from him, he did not know whether his turn lights worked. Therefore, although he knew he used his turn signal, he did not know until a year and a half later that his lights were indeed working.

The court ruled that there was still no reason Rosado could not have sued within the two-year period as he had the video six months before the statute of limitations ran out.

Wiley v Chicago, 361 F3d 994 (7th Cir, 2003)
Wiley was arrested January 2000. His case was dismissed July 2002. Wiley brought suit for false arrest/wrongful prosecution in August 2002.

The Seventh Circuit Court of Appeals ruled that Wiley's false arrest claim did not violate the statute of limitations.

II. Procedures and Remedies

Civil rights remedies spring from numerous sources. This book focuses primarily on complaints related to Section 1983 actions founded on Fourth, Fifth, Sixth, and Fourteenth Amendment violations. This section explains in a very general way how the procedure works for Section 1983 actions.

Categorizing tort actions against police

There are a number of ways to look at civil rights remedies. One way is to think about unconstitutional (unreasonable) searches and seizures or unconstitutional interrogations. Another way is to think according to other categorical variables or causes of action, such as common law torts. When a citizen sues under common law, he/she must prove that the officer's conduct was at least "wanton and willful." This book in general deals only with constitutional torts, but the last part discusses, rather briefly and summarily, common law torts.

Stating the specific constitutional violation

The Supreme Court has explained that, since Section 1983 doesn't specify what particular rights are being protected, the plaintiff must specify exactly what constitutional right has been violated and why. That is the reason why the courts have switched to a Fourth Amendment (or sometimes Fifth, Sixth, or Fourteenth Amendment) analysis when deciding these types of cases.

Civil procedure

Civil procedure can be very complicated. This section will explain (relatively superficially) the fundamentals of the civil process as it relates to Section 1983 actions:

- First, the plaintiff must claim that the defendant violated a constitutional right of the plaintiff [BAKER V MCCOLLAN, 443 US 137 (1970)].
- Second, the defendant's lawyer files a response. Often the lawyer seeks summary judgment or dismissal based on qualified immunity. Summary judgment means that, even if everything the plaintiff says is true, the plaintiff does not have a cause of action. A court will assume for purposes of this ruling that the basic complaint and affidavits filed by the plaintiff are true. If partial summary judgment is granted, there must be a determination as to whether there is any issue left to be litigated. Often summary judgment is sought based on qualified immunity. The qualified immunity defense can (and probably should) be presented very early in the process.
- Third, if summary judgment—based on the fact that the officer(s) did nothing wrong constitutionally—is denied, the defense attorney for the officer(s) might plead for protection for the officer under the doctrine of qualified immunity. This basically means that, although the officer may arguably have violated the plaintiff's constitutional rights, the law was not settled on the issue at the time of the violation such that the reasonable officer would know that he/she committed a violation.
- Fourth, if the court finds that the plaintiff does have a cause of action and the above motions are denied, the case normally proceeds to trial or settlement.
- Fifth, if the case goes to trial, and if during the trial or at the end of the trial the defense attorney can prove to the court that the plaintiff's facts do not rise to the level of a constitutional violation, the defense attorney can ask the judge to grant a verdict for the defense.
- Sixth, if the plaintiff can show intentional or malicious-type misconduct (usually excessive force) by officers, the plaintiff can seek punitive damages which usually must be paid by the officers themselves.
- Seventh, the party who "prevails" may get attorney's fees from the defeated party.

III. Summary Judgment

Summary judgment is sought by an attorney who believes that, even conceding the other side's facts are correct, the other side must lose as a matter of law without ever going to trial. Often the defense/officer will seek summary judgment and the plaintiff will seek summary judgment as to certain issues.

Qualified immunity: timing

Sometimes the courts grant summary judgment, and the Supreme Court has held that the decision as to whether or not an officer deserves to be granted qualified immunity and summary judgment in such cases should be addressed early in the process so that the officer is not required to defend himself through a long drawn-out court battle, if he deserves immunity for his conduct.

Difference between summary judgment and qualified immunity

Without getting academic or technical, qualified immunity is summary judgment as qualified immunity means that the litigant, usually the officer, does not have to go to trial. The important difference for officers in the future is that officers reading past cases where the court awarded summary judgment (stating that the officer did nothing unconstitutional), can rely on that, whereas qualified immunity has traditionally meant the opposite.

Dockery v Blackburn and Higgins, 911 F.3d 458 (7th Cir. 2018)
Officers lawfully arrested Dockery after a domestic incident, where Dockery, while allegedly high on PCP, broke into his girlfriend's apartment after being banned from the complex. He proceeded to punch holes in the wall and destroy property.

The officers eventually took Dockery to the police department. During booking, which was videotaped both by the video in the room and subsequently by a Taser, Dockery's handcuffs were removed. During the fingerprinting, Dockery (playfully?) tapped Officer Higgins on the shoulder twice and then grabbed Higgins' shoulder and shook it. Higgins told Dockery he would be handcuffed for the rest of the process. Dockery folded his arms and stepped toward Higgins. Higgins pulled Dockery's arm behind his back and led him toward a bench. At that point, Dockery began to physically resist all attempts to restrain him.

Sgt. Blackburn, who was sitting at a desk in the room, pulled out her Taser. Dockery, who was at least three inches taller and 100 pounds heavier than Blackburn, began to approach her. Blackburn tased Dockery, but one of the prongs was damaged or detached. Blackburn applied the Taser directly to Dockery's back. Dockery continued to resist. During this period, Dockery kicked out at the officers. Finally, four officers managed to control and handcuff Dockery. Ultimately, it appears that Dockery was tased at least four times.

Dockery sued the officers under Section 1983, arguing that he fell because he was overweight, did not even resist the officers, his arms were painfully wrenched behind his back, and the officers handcuffed him too tight (as Dockery had lacerations from the handcuffs on his wrists).

The federal district court judge ruled that the officers did not deserve qualified immunity as Dockery argued that his conduct was innocent even within the context of the video. He simply was being playful to start, he fell down, and his kicking action and rolling were involuntary as he had been tased. (These actions were very threatening and should have been documented as such.)

The Seventh Circuit ruled that the video reflected that Dockery did make aggressive moves toward the officers during the attempts to handcuff him (active resistance and threat).

Previous case law reflected that when an arrested suspect is "kicking or flailing," Clarett v Roberts, 657 F3d 664 (7th Cir 2011) or "declining to follow [lawful] directions while acting in a belligerent manner," Forrest v Prine, 620 F3d 739 (7th Cir 2010) the use of a Taser does not constitute excessive force.

Therefore, the officers deserved qualified immunity.

> *But why not exoneration? Did the officers violate Dockery's rights or not? It would seem that the court could have said (should have said?), "No." See MENA below.*

When summary judgment is appropriate
Summary judgment may be granted the officer (or the plaintiff) when there is no dispute as to the facts, and the facts reflect that there is no constitutional violation (or that there is an obvious violation the officer should have known about)—or as a matter of law, the court can rule that the officer did violate the plaintiff's rights.

Summary judgment by qualified immunity can be awarded when there was no case or doctrine on point that would have put the officer(s) on notice that what they were doing was arguably unconstitutional.

In either case, summary judgment may only occur when the defendant/officer concedes, for purposes of the motion, that the plaintiff's facts are true and then argues or even concedes that the defendant did not violate the plaintiff's rights.

MUEHLER V MENA, 544 US 93 (2005)

Swat team officers executed a search warrant at a home where the officers were aware that violent gang members lived and hung out. The warrant authorized the officers to search for a weapon and drugs, among other things.

The only person at the home at the time of the execution was Iris Mena. She was awakened in bed by officers with guns drawn. She was handcuffed and taken in the "pouring" rain to the garage. Mena was confined to the garage for about three hours while the SWAT team searched the house. (The SWAT team located three other "suspects" in trailers behind the house. They were also handcuffed and confined in the garage.) Two officers stood watch over the "detainees." During the detention, immigration officers questioned Mena about her immigration status.

No evidence of criminal activity was located in Mena's room.

Mena sued the officers under Section 1983 for violating her Fourth Amendment right to be free from unreasonable seizures.

The trial court (the Federal District court) denied the officers' motion for summary judgment or qualified immunity. So the case went to trial—by jury. The jury decided that the officers violated Mena's rights and awarded her both compensatory and (substantial) punitive damages (which officers are required to pay personally).

The Federal Court of Appeals agreed that neither summary judgment nor qualified immunity was appropriate, since the officers obviously detained Mena unconstitutionally by keeping her handcuffed for about three hours and questioning her about issues having nothing to do with the warrant, i.e. her immigration status.

The United States Supreme Court reversed, holding that the officers did not violate Mena's Fourth Amendment rights in any way (even while conceding the truth of Mena's facts). The Court reasoned that when officers reasonably believe that weapons are involved in the search for evidence, it is reasonable to keep occupants handcuffed during the execution of the warrant. Also, questioning detainees is not unconstitutional unless the time period for the questioning exceeds the time it takes to execute the warrant. Therefore, summary judgment should have been awarded to the officers.

Jones v Wilhelm, 425 F3d 455 (2005)

A search warrant ordered the search of the apartment on the "right" at the top of the stairs. The officer in charge of executing the warrant thought that the warrant meant the "left" at the top of the stairs. There were a number of reasons for this mistake, one of them being that there were two staircases facing in opposite directions leading up to the apartments. So the officers entered the wrong apartment (the Jones' apartment). When they learned that they were in the wrong apartment, they apologized, quickly left, and searched the right apartment.

The Seventh Circuit Court of Appeals ruled that the officers should have cleared up the facial ambiguity in the warrant before serving it, and, therefore, they were not entitled to qualified immunity on the warrant claim.

The court then held that the plaintiffs deserved summary judgment on their claim in that "Wilhelm's decision then to proceed with the execution of a search warrant he knew to be ambiguous violated the Jones' Fourth Amendment rights... There is no genuine issue of fact."

Dawson v Brown, 803 F3d 829 (7th Cir 2015)
Officers were arresting Dawson's son after he fled from officers during the officer's attempt to execute a traffic stop. During the struggle on Dawson's driveway, Dawson approached the officers and "showed his hands" indicating that he did not have a weapon. An officer deployed his taser on the son, but it didn't work. He was about to deploy it again when the father came within three or four feet of the fight and said, "Please don't kill him." He also put his hand on an officer and told him, "Leave my son alone. Don't hurt him." The officer told Dawson to get back and kicked Dawson in the side. Dawson stumbled backward and was then tackled by another officer.

Dawson was arrested for resisting and obstruction. But he was never formally charged. He went to the emergency room for injuries he sustained.

Dawson filed six counts against the officer(s) under Section 1983, mostly related to excessive force.

The Seventh Circuit Court of Appeals ruled that there were no material facts at issue. Therefore, the case could be settled as a matter of law. It was reasonable for the officer to "believe that Dawson was attempting to interfere with a lawful arrest." Therefore, the officers were granted summary judgment.

Fuller v Vines, 36 F3d 65 (1994)
Officers were lawfully investigating an incident when they passed by Fuller's front yard. The officers said that Fuller's dog Champ charged at the officers, so the officers shot and killed the dog. Fuller testified that when he objected to the officer's shooting his dog, an officer pointed the gun at Fuller's head and threatened to kill him by stating that he (the officer) was going to send Fuller "to the morgue" with the clear implication to back off. The officers then left.

Fuller sued under Section 1983.

The Ninth Circuit Court of Appeals ruled that there was no seizure in the constitutional sense in that Fuller was free to leave and was in fact told to leave. According to everyone, there was no arrest or TERRY stop. The officer was simply taking no chances that Fuller would attack him (the officer). Therefore, according to the Ninth Circuit, summary judgment was properly granted.

This does not mean that you cannot be sued under some other cause of action, e.g. due process or common law. It simply means that you cannot be liable for an unconstitutional seizure when there was no seizure. So even given the truth of the plaintiff's facts, the case must be dismissed.

Billington v Smith, 292 F3d 1177 (2002)
Officer Smith, while driving with his family in plainclothes, saw Hennessey driving recklessly at speeds of 70 mph on a 30-35 mph street. The officer turned on his emergency equipment and chased Hennessey briefly. Hennessey crashed into a curb. Smith went up to render aid. The officer then identified himself and determined that Hennessey, who had a BAC of .285, should be arrested. Hennessey, instead, decided to drive away, but the car was too damaged to move.

Hennessey then began to fight with the officer. Witnesses said that Hennessey was the aggressor and that Hennessey continued to attack with kicks and blows, even when the officer backed off. The officer finally shot Hennessey and killed him.

The witnesses who saw the shooting differed in their recollections. Some stated that Hennessey was getting the upper hand when the officer pushed Hennessey a few feet away and shot him. Others said Hennessey was closer than three feet. The officer maintained that he shot Hennessey as they struggled for the officer's gun. Ballistics tests showed that gun was 8 to 14 inches from Hennessey when the officer shot him.

The district court refused to grant summary judgment.

The Ninth Circuit Court of Appeals ruled that, even if the witnesses were correct and the officer was wrong, there was no material factual difference. The court ruled that "Detective Smith could have reasonably shot Hennessey even if he had just pushed Hennessey a few feet away." Therefore, summary judgment in favor of the officer was appropriate.

When summary judgment / qualified immunity is not appropriate—factual disputes

If there is a material factual dispute, the case should go to trial as only a jury can decide a factual dispute.

TOLAN V COTTON, 134 S Ct 1861 (2014)

An officer saw two young men get out of their car on a residential street at 2 a.m. One of them was Tolan. The officer ran the license plate. The officer entered the wrong license number by mistake, and the car came back stolen.

The officer told the two occupants to get on the ground, and they complied. The officer said the car was stolen. Tolan tried to explain that he did not steal the car. Tolan's parents came out of the house and told the police that the car belonged to them. Both parents told the occupants to stay on the ground. Tolan's father told police that the "kids" were his son and nephew. Both parents said this was a "big mistake" as the "car was not stolen."

Officer Cotton arrived at the scene and drew his pistol. He ordered the mother to move to the garage door. She responded, "Are you kidding me? We have lived here 15 years, and nothing like this has ever happened before." Tolan's mother later testified that Cotton grabbed her arm and slammed her against the garage door. Tolan's mother had pictures of the bruises, etc., that resulted.

Tolan then rose to his knees and yelled for the officer to "get your f____ hands off my mom." Cotton shot Tolan three times resulting in life-altering injuries. Cotton (and other officers) testified that Tolan was on his feet and that he feared Tolan was coming after him.

The Federal District Court granted summary judgment for Cotton. In reaching that decision the court relied, in part, on the following factors disputed by Tolan:

- The front porch was dimly lit.
- Tolan's mother had refused orders to remain calm and quiet.
- Tolan's mother refused to move to the garage and pulled away from the officer.
- Tolan's words amounted to a "verbal threat."
- Tolan was "moving to intervene" in Cotton's handling of Tolan's mother.

The United States Supreme Court reversed, ruling that if a lower court is going to grant summary judgment, the court must accept the facts of the non-moving party when there are material disputes over facts. In this case the factual disputes must be decided by a jury.

The Court stated that the Court of Appeals failed to view evidence "in a light most favorable to Tolan with respect to the central facts of this case." The Tolans testified:

1. The porch was not dimly lit and that two flood lights provided a lot of light for the officer to see that Tolan was on his knees.
2. Tolan testified that he was in the light when shot—not in darkness.
3. Tolan (and his mother) insisted that she was calm during her pleas to the officers.
4. Tolan admitted that he said, "Get your f______ hands off my mom." But his words were simply stated as a plea not to continue any assault of his mother. They were not stated as a threat.
5. Tolan and his family testified that Tolan was on his knees—that he did not stand up before being shot.

The Supreme Court then stated that the lower court should have "acknowledged and credited Tolan's evidence with regard to the lighting, his mother's demeanor, whether he shouted words that were an overt threat, and his positioning during the shooting" as the party not moving for summary judgment always gets the benefit of the doubt as to disputed facts.

Therefore, only a jury can decide the material "facts"—and determine who is telling the truth.

Alexander v City and County of San Francisco, 29 F3d 1355 (1994)
Public health officials obtained an inspection warrant to investigate a sewage leak at a house. When they attempted to serve the warrant, a man inside said that he was going to "get (his) gun and use it." The SWAT team was called in. The SWAT team broke into the house. The man tried to shoot at the SWAT team (but his gun misfired). The SWAT team then shot and killed the man.

The Ninth Circuit Court of Appeals ruled that the officers did not have a warrant (arrest or search), consent, or exigency to enter the premises before the shooting. Therefore, there was no justification for a summary judgment in favor of the officers, as was awarded by the district court.

Hopkins v Andaya, 958 F2d 881 (1992)
Officer Andaya was called to Capri Hotel in response to a person, Hopkins, who was causing a disturbance and threatening to "shoot the place up." The officer determined that the suspect was unarmed and not a danger to anyone, so he released him. The suspect then began to bray or howl at a traffic light. When he started to walk back toward the hotel, Andaya decided to stop him.

During the confrontation, Andaya said that Hopkins took Andaya's baton away and started to hit him (the officer) around the head and shoulders. Andaya then shot Hopkins six times. Apparently, during this period also, Hopkins (after being shot) chased the officer across the street, where the officer shot him four times.

A witness, however, stated that Hopkins never had Andaya's baton, and that as soon as Andaya fell, he (Andaya) shot Hopkins. No warning was ever given. The witness further stated that Andaya was on his feet when he fired the last shot. Hopkins died.

The district court awarded summary judgment for Andaya, but the Ninth Circuit Court of Appeals reversed, stating that Andaya's hospital records tended to show that he was not hit (by Hopkins) where he said he was, and that the witness' statement appeared to be more accurate than Andaya's. The court deduced that, if Hopkins had been shot five times and Anaya was on his feet for the last shot, a jury could conclude that the force exhibited was excessive. In fact, there was evidence that the officer may have shot four times after Hopkins was wounded and greatly incapacitated.

Finally, the Ninth Circuit ruled that summary judgment for the city and the chief were inappropriate in this case, as "the police chief and the city might be held liable for improper training or improper procedure even if Andaya is exonerated, since as the court stated, 'They put an officer on the street who is so badly trained and instructed he lets his baton be taken away from him and then has to kill an unarmed civilian to save his own life. Andaya has a history of citizen complaints of excessive force, a reputation for being quick-tempered, and has drawn or fired his gun inappropriately several times before. These facts certainly bear on whether the city properly trained Andaya and whether they should have sent him out on the streets carrying a weapon.'"

Hansen v Black, 885 F2d 642 (1989)
Officers responded to a robbery. The footprints in the snow from the robbery led the officers to Hansen's residence. Two officers watched the house while other officers went to get a warrant.

According to the police, in the morning Kathleen Hansen came out of her home with garbage and began to put the garbage in the garbage truck. The officers started to take the garbage from the truck, and Hansen tried to stop them. Officer Black told Hansen that, if she didn't stop hindering him she would be arrested. Hansen then looked at the officer and said, "Son of a bitch." Hansen was then arrested.

Hansen, on the other hand, filed an affidavit that said she did not physically or verbally hinder the officers from removing the garbage from the truck. She stated also that she was at least 75 feet from the officers. Finally she said "son of a bitch" to the mounds of garbage that had not been removed from her driveway.

A neighbor filed an affidavit that stated that the officers were in a different driveway from Hansen when all the talk went on and that there was a garbage man between Hansen and the officers.

The district court granted summary judgment for the officers.

The Ninth Circuit Court of Appeals reversed the district court's ruling that there was no genuine issue of material fact, stating that there was a genuine factual dispute and held that the facts could only be resolved by a jury.

Strand v Minchuk, 910 F3d 909 (2018)
An officer and a truck driver got into a fist fight over parking tickets. The officer shot the truck driver. The truck driver (plaintiff) said that when he was shot, he had put up his hands and capitulated. The truck driver sued under Section 1983.

The district court judge ruled that the case must go to a jury and that under the plaintiff's facts, the officer unconstitutionally shot the truck driver.

The Seventh Circuit ruled that the officer cannot be awarded qualified immunity if the truck driver had raised his hands and gave up, saying, "I surrender, I'm done."

IV. Seizures

Most Section 1983 cases filed against officers are brought because citizens complain that officers used unreasonable force during a seizure. There are also numerous cases where officers arrested suspects without probable cause; some cases where officers detained suspects without reasonable suspicion and only a few related to the seizure of property (because the "issue" when dealing with property is almost always a "search" question).

Seizures of persons

Officers are sued mainly for unconstitutional seizures when the officers:

- Take suspects into custody without probable cause (most of these are also supported by a state charge of false imprisonment);
- Use unreasonable/excessive force while detaining or taking a suspect into custody.

Officers must have reasonable suspicion to detain a suspect. Many of these encounters are also characterized as, or escalate into, false imprisonment or false arrest.

The following is a discussion of the seizure issues incrementally rising from restraints to unreasonable and excessive force used during and after an arrest. Remember, even if a defendant is convicted of murder, he can still sue for excessive force in the arrest. Evans v Poskon, 603 F3d 362 (2010)

Much of this will follow the order of the second chapter in Volume I.

Pre-seizure tactics and conduct

Plaintiffs often argue that, if the officer had executed better pre-seizure tactics, there would have been no need for the amount of force used. Usually this occurs in shootings, but it can arise in many other settings.

The main rule is that, if the officer creates the problem, sometimes the officer's creation of the risk can result in liability when the officer uses deadly force only because of the risk created by the officer's poor judgment [Estate of Stark v Emhart, 5 F3d 230 (1993)].

How this question is resolved is crucial for officers. If "expert" witnesses are allowed to testify to juries that the officers in the case did something "unwise" BEFORE the force was used—and that had they done something wise/different, the victim would not be dead or hurt, etc., officers are going to be second-guessed until the second coming. See the cases below, and you will understand this issue fully.

SAN FRANCISCO V SHEEHAN, 135 S Ct 1765 (2015)

Sheehan lived in a room in a facility for people with mental illnesses. A social worker stopped in to see Sheehan in her room, as Sheehan had stopped taking her medication and was no longer changing her clothes or eating. Sheehan told the social worker that she had a knife and would kill him if he didn't leave.

The social worker left and called the police. The social worker then sought—and received—help to get Sheehan to a hospital for treatment as she was obviously a danger to other people.

An officer arrived but realized quickly that she needed backup and called her sergeant. The two of them entered Sheehan's room after knocking and announcing their purpose. They told her when they knocked that they wanted to help her. Sheehan grabbed a 5-inch kitchen knife and told the officers that she was going to kill them. The officers retreated out of the room, and Sheehan closed the door.

The officers heard sirens, indicating more backup was on the way. The officers decided to immediately re-enter and subdue Sheehan before backup arrived. The officers entered Sheehan's room with pistols drawn. The sergeant immediately pepper sprayed Sheehan. When Sheehan attacked the officers with a knife, the officers shot her.

The prosecutor could not get a conviction against Sheehan. Sheehan sued under Section 1983 for entering her room without a warrant and excessive force.

The Federal District Court ruled that the officers should be accorded summary judgment on the exigency issue because they had to act quickly in that they didn't know if:

- Sheehan would go out the back window (although she was on the second floor) or
- Whether there was someone else in Sheehan's room whom Sheehan might harm or
- Whether she might hurt herself.

The court further held that the shooting was justified as Sheehan represented a threat of death or great bodily injury to the officers.

The Ninth Circuit Court of Appeals reversed, ruling that there was "no objective need for immediate entry." The Ninth Circuit also decided that the officers "provoked" the response from Sheehan. Finally, the court held that the officers had been put on notice by numerous Ninth Circuit cases that told the officers that their conduct was unconstitutional.

The United States Supreme Court basically agreed with the District Court on the facts supporting the emergency entry; but ruling that, even if the officers were wrong, they deserved qualified immunity, concluding that everyone has 20/20 hindsight and that it's easy to second guess officers in this very tense circumstance. Finally, the Court ruled that the officers deserved qualified immunity as there were no cases directly on point that would have put the officers on notice that they were doing anything unconstitutional.

Estate of Starks v Enyart, 5 F3d 230 (7th Cir 1993)
Starks stole a taxi cab. He parked in a Taco Bell parking lot. Three officers approached Starks. According to an independent eye witness, Starks attempted to drive off going forward. He had a very narrow path to escape beside a utility pole. An officer jumped out from behind the utility pole into the narrow path in front of Stark's car and shot Starks. The other officers shot Starks too.

The Federal District ruled that the officers should get summary judgment as Starks represented a threat of serious bodily injury or death, so deadly force was justified.

The Seventh Circuit ruled that the officer put himself in harm's way and, therefore, did not deserve summary judgment. The Seventh Circuit held that it was the officer's fault that the officer was in a situation where deadly force must be used and, therefore, a case of poor pre-seizure strategy. (See Billington below, a Ninth Circuit case for a different look at this issue).

Billington v Smith, 292 F3d 1177 (2002)
Officer Smith, while driving with his family in plainclothes, saw Hennessey driving recklessly at speeds of 70 mph on a 30-35 mph street. The officer turned on his emergency equipment and chased Hennessey briefly. Hennessey crashed into a curb. Smith went up to render aid. The officer identified himself and determined that Hennessey (who had a BAC of .285%) should be arrested. Hennessey, instead, decided to drive away, but the car was too damaged to move.

Hennessey then began to fight with the officer. Witnesses said that Hennessey was the aggressor and that Hennessey continued to attack with kicks and blows even when the officer backed off. The officer shot Hennessey and killed him.

The plaintiff called an expert witness (a retired police chief) who testified that it was unreasonable:

- For the officer to be in a squad car with his wife and daughter
- For him to get out of his car without a backup
- For him to approach the suspect without handcuffs, spray, or a first aid kit
- That he did not release the magazine from his gun to disarm it
- That he was unable to subdue a smaller drunk man without shooting him

Hennessey's estate argued that the officer "created the need to use such force" by virtue of his pre-seizure conduct and failure to act reasonably.

The district court refused to grant summary judgment on the issues of the officer's failure to drop off his family, failure to await a backup, failure to use a baton or spray.

The Ninth Circuit Court of Appeals ruled that none of the officer's "supposed errors could be deemed intentional or reckless, much less unconstitutional, provocations that caused Hennessey to attack him." Therefore, summary judgment in favor of the officer was appropriate.

Alexander v City and County of San Francisco, 29 F3d 1355 (1994)
Public health officials obtained an inspection warrant to investigate a sewage leak at a house. When they attempted to serve the warrant, a man inside said that he was going to "get (his) gun and use it." The SWAT team was called in. The SWAT team broke into the house. The man tried to shoot the SWAT team (but his gun misfired). The SWAT team then shot and killed the man.

The Ninth Circuit Court of Appeals ruled that the officers did not have a warrant (arrest or search), consent, or exigency to enter the premises before the shooting. So since the pre-seizure strategy was flawed, the officers acted unconstitutionally (even though the shooting itself appeared justified). Therefore, there was no justification for a summary judgment in favor of the officers.

Seizures versus non-seizures
In order to trigger liability for an unconstitutional seizure, there must be a seizure in the first place. This section will discuss the cases where the courts ruled that there either was or was not a seizure in a civil case.

General rule
If a citizen is not free to leave, the suspect is seized. If the suspect is free to leave, the suspect is not seized.

Non-seizures
The following are circumstances where the courts ruled that there was no seizure under the Fourth Amendment.

SACRAMENTO V LEWIS, 118 S Ct 1708 (1998)
Officers chased the driver of a motorcycle who was driving recklessly and speeding. The motorcycle missed a turn and the passenger, Lewis, was killed.

The United States Supreme Court ruled that the motorcycle driver and passenger were not seized in that they did not stop nor were they stopped by the officers. Therefore, Lewis had no cause of action against Sacramento.

Cameron v Pontiac, 813 F2d 782 (1987)
Officers responded to a burglary and saw two burglars fleeing. One burglar stopped, but the other one, Cameron, escaped over a fence. The officers shot at the burglar, but missed. Cameron ran into the street and was killed by a vehicle. Cameron's estate sued.

The federal court ruled that there was no seizure. Therefore, there could be no constitutional tort.

Fuller v Vines, 36 F3d 65 (1994)
Officers were lawfully investigating an incident when they passed by Fuller's front yard. The officers said that Fuller's dog, Champ, charged at the officers, so the officers shot and killed the dog. Fuller was so upset that a friend had to restrain him.

Fuller said when he objected to the officers about the shooting of the dog, an officer pointed a gun at Fuller's head and threatened to kill him, stating that he (the officer) was going to send Fuller "to the morgue." The officers then left.

Fuller sued under Section 1983.

The Ninth Circuit Court of Appeals ruled that there was no seizure in the constitutional sense in that Fuller was free to leave. (In fact, the officer was implying that Fuller must back off or leave.) According to everyone, there was no arrest or TERRY stop. The officer was simply taking no chances that Fuller would attack him (the officer). Therefore, summary judgment was properly granted, as there could be no constitutional violation under the circumstances.

> *This does not mean the officer cannot be sued under another cause of action—just that if there is no seizure, there can be no Fourth Amendment violation.*

McCoy v Harrison, 341 F3d 600 (2003)
An officer got information that McCoy's dogs were being abused. The officer had been to McCoy's before and knew she had 20 to 30 dogs and sold them without a license.

When the officer went onto McCoy's property, McCoy told him to get off her property. As the officer started to open the gate to look at the dogs and take pictures, McCoy tried to shut the gate. The officer backhanded her in the face, and she fell to the ground.

The Seventh Circuit Court of Appeals ruled that the officer "made no effort to direct or impede her movements." Therefore, there was no seizure and no Fourth Amendment violation.

White v Markham, 310 F3d 989 (2002)
White lived with his son in his aunt's house. White did not pay rent, but he agreed to perform chores, pay utility bills and protect the property in return for living in the home rent-free. The parties agreed informally that White would move out sometime after April 1. On March 8, the owner/aunt told White that he would have to get out. An argument ensued, and White called the police.

When an officer arrived, he saw that many items of property had been broken. Both parties asked the officer to throw the other party out of the house. The officer finally decided to throw White out. The officer put his hand on White's shoulder and told him that if he did not leave immediately, he would be arrested. White said he didn't want to leave and asked the officer to call his attorney. The officer refused. After repeated threats to arrest, White and his son left the house. White's attorney later called the chief of police, but the chief refused to intervene.

Two months later White filed a Section 1983 action alleging, among other things, deprivation of Fourth Amendment rights.

The Seventh Circuit Court of Appeals ruled that White and his son "were free to leave at any time." Therefore, there could be no seizure. Therefore, there could be no Fourth Amendment violation.

The Court believed that there might have been a seizure (technically) in that the officer touched White and ordered him around. The Court also held that, if there was a seizure, the seizure was reasonable. Also, although there was no seizure here, White may have had a different cause of action.

Don't confuse this with (unlawful) eviction proceedings.

Seizures
The following are the cases where the courts ruled there was a seizure.

BROWER V COUNTY OF INYO, 489 US 593 (1989)
Officers set up a roadblock to stop Brower. Brower ran his vehicle into the roadblock and was hurt.

The United States Supreme Court, using Fourth Amendment analysis, ruled that the roadblock was a seizure and that the seizure was unreasonable. Therefore, Brower had a cause of action.

SCOTT V HARRIS, 127 S Ct 1209 (2007)
Deputy Scott chased Harris at speeds nearing 90 mph. Scott then intentionally bumped Harris' vehicle causing the vehicle to spin out of control. As a result, Harris' vehicle crashed, and Harris was rendered quadriplegic. Harris sued under Section 1983.

The United States Supreme Court ruled that the officer's bumping Harris' vehicle was a seizure.

The Court further held that the seizure was deadly force applied constitutionally, because Scott posed a substantial immediate risk of serious bodily injury to others on the road.

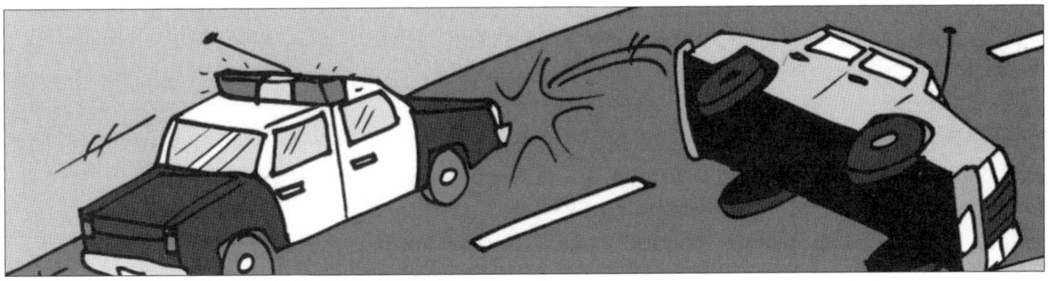

People v McGann, 8 F3d 1174 (1993)
Officers searched every car leaving a Metra (Railroad) employee parking lot. A sign when entering the lot indicated that all cars were subject to search. Employees sued because there was no safe place to park cars near the lot. Also, employees testified that they thought that officers would search only with a reason. Officers tried to argue that the employees were not stopped/seized—that employees were free to leave.

The Seventh Circuit Court of Appeals ruled that the officers did seize the employees (and there was a question of fact about whether the employees consented by implication to the search). Therefore, the employees had a cause of action against the police and Metra.

Stops with or without reasonable suspicion

It is a constitutional violation creating a cause of action when an officer stops (seizes) a driver of a vehicle or a pedestrian without at least reasonable suspicion (unless there is some exception to the rule which the officer can proffer).

Giddeon v Flynn, 830 F3d 719 (2016)
Giddeon's former girlfriend reported to the police that Giddeon had attacked her in her home and threatened to shoot her. Later, officers saw a woman leaving the victim's home and getting into a car with five other occupants. The officers stopped the car and then determined that one of the occupants, a passenger, was Giddeon. The officers handcuffed Giddeon and put him in the back seat of the patrol car.

The driver of the car consented to a search of the vehicle. During the search, the officers found a gun, which was in a shopping bag and wrapped in clothing. The bag belonged to Giddeon's sister. His sister told police that the gun belonged to her brother.

The officers told Giddeon about the gun, and Giddeon admitted the gun was his. Subsequently, Giddeon pled guilty to being a felon in possession of a firearm and was sentenced to five years in prison and five years of supervised release.

Giddeon sued under Section 1983 asserting that the seizure was unconstitutional as the police did not have probable cause to stop the car. The officers conceded that they did not have enough evidence / suspicion to stop the car.

The Seventh Circuit ruled that the stop was unconstitutional. Therefore, Giddeon was entitled to damages. As the court stated, "They may well be nominal, but he is entitled to a hearing in the district court to determine their amount."

Davis v Novy, 433 F3d 926 (2006)
An anonymous caller told police that there was a man, apparently in a truck, taking pictures of little girls. An officer followed a truck that was close to the description of the suspect's truck. The officer noticed that the registration sticker was obscured so he pulled the driver (Davis) over.

The officer asked for, and apparently obtained, consent to search the truck. The officer discovered various items (including a woman's thong, a camera, and court documents out of South Dakota) that aroused his suspicions. The officers then asked for consent to search Davis' home. Davis consented. The officers found nothing of concern in the home and, therefore, wrote Davis up for vehicle violations and told Davis he was free to leave. Davis had been detained for two hours.

Davis sued for seizing him without probable cause.

The Seventh Circuit Court of Appeals ruled that the anonymous tip (probably) did not create reasonable suspicion for the stop, but the obscured sticker did create probable cause for the traffic stop. Therefore, the court held that summary judgment in favor of the officers was appropriate.

Buffkins v Omaha, 922 F2d 465 (1990)
An anonymous tipster told police that a black person would be bringing drugs in on a certain plane from Denver. Police observed that there was only one black person on the plane, a female named Buffkins. The

officers observed that she appeared nervous and carried a teddy bear that appeared to have been re-sewn.

The officers confronted Buffkins, took her luggage and escorted Buffkins to the office on the other side of the terminal. At the security office, the officers obtained Buffkins' license and ticket. The officers asked if they could search her bags, and Buffkins refused permission. The officers checked out the teddy bear, but determined that it did not contain drugs. Eventually the officers told Buffkins that she was free to leave. Buffkins responded by calling the officer an "asshole" or said something about the "asshole system" as she was walking out the door. The officers then arrested her for disorderly conduct.

The district court ruled that there was no unconstitutional seizure, but the Court of Appeals reversed, ruling that there was no reasonable suspicion to support the seizure. The case was remanded for trial.

White v Markham, 310 F3d 989 (2002)
White lived with his son in his aunt's house. White did not pay rent, but he agreed to perform chores, pay utility bills and protect the property in return for living in the home rent-free. The parties agreed informally that White would move out sometime after April 1. On March 8, the owner/aunt told White that he would have to get out. An argument ensued and White called the police.

When an officer arrived he saw that many items of property had been broken. Both parties asked the officer to throw the other party out of the house. The officer finally decided to throw White out. The officer put his hand on White's shoulder and told him that if he did not leave immediately, he would be arrested. White said he didn't want to leave and asked the officer to call his attorney. The officer refused. After repeated threats to arrest, White and his son left the house. White's attorney later called the chief of police, but the chief refused to intervene.

Two months later White filed a Section 1983 action alleging, among other things, deprivation of Fourth Amendment rights.

The Seventh Circuit Court of Appeals ruled that whether or not White was even seized was a close question. But that if White was, in fact, seized, the seizure was probably reasonable even though the officer was without reasonable suspicion (creating a sort of exception to reasonable suspicion rule). Finally, the court held that even if there was no reasonable suspicion, the officers deserved qualified immunity in this very tough situation.

Ford v Wilson, 90 F3d 245 (1996)
An officer stopped Ford on a traffic offense and later arrested Ford. Ford brought a lawsuit alleging that the officer did not have any reason for stopping Ford, except that Ford was black.

The federal court of appeals ruled that the basis of the complaint was not the constitutionality of the traffic stop, but that the officer stopped Ford because he was black. Therefore, the case was dismissed.

Arrests/custody with or without probable cause

Officers must understand that they cannot take suspects into custody/arrest them without probable cause.

The problem is that everyone has a different idea of what probable cause is. Technically, probable cause is not a "more-than-likely" test. If you think of a water bucket totally full of water as proof beyond a reasonable doubt, then probable cause is water slightly less than half full. The United States Supreme Court has explained its definition of probable cause many times as reflected in Volume I. Even judges on the Supreme Court disagree on whether a particular set of facts constitutes probable cause.

In some of the following cases, the officers were granted qualified immunity because, even though there was no probable cause to arrest, there was at the time no case that put the officer on notice that probable cause did not exist.

DISTRICT OF COLUMBIA V WESBY, 138 S Ct 577 (2018)
Officers responded to a noisy party call. The caller said that the house had been vacant for months. Neighbors said the same. Officers entered the house. The officers could immediately see that the house was filthy and had very little furniture. Most of the 21 partiers thought it was a bachelor's party but didn't know who the bachelor was. Virtually all of them said they were invited. Two females said that Peaches had invited them. But Peaches eventually admitted that she did not have permission to use it. The owner stated that the partiers did not have the owner's permission to be there. The officers then arrested the partiers, but the prosecutor dismissed the case.

The partiers sued under Section 1983 for false arrest as the partiers all felt they were in the house lawfully.

Both the district court and court of appeals ruled that there was no evidence of intent. Therefore, there was no probable cause, and the arrests were unconstitutional.

The United States Supreme Court reversed, ruling there was probable cause because of the condition of the house and the conduct of the party-goers, including hiding and their vague answers. Though the Court appeared to find probable cause, the Court also decided that the officers deserved qualified immunity.

The following are numerous cases where officers were sued for failure to possess probable cause when they "arrested" suspects, held them beyond the period of detention, etc. [See e.g. RODRIGUEZ V UNITED STATES, 135 S. Ct. 1609 (2015) .]

NIEVES V BARTLETT, 139 S Ct 1715 (2019)
Trooper Nieves was looking for underaged drinkers at a large outdoor party in Alaska. He went up to talk to Bartlett. Bartlett told the officer, "I don't want to talk to you."

Later, Trooper Weight was talking to a minor. Bartlett told Trooper Weight that the officer did not "have the authority to talk to M.W. [the minor] without a parent or guardian present." At that time Bartlett was face to face with Trooper Weight and the minor was to the right of Bartlett. (This was on video.) Weight said, "No," and pushed Bartlett backwards. Bartlett's hands went up (apparently in reaction). Trooper Nieves saw this, grabbed Bartlett's arm and yelled, "Back up!" Trooper Weight grabbed Bartlett's other arm. Both officers repeatedly yelled for Bartlett to get on the ground. Bartlett hesitated as he had a bad back. The officers threatened Bartlett with a Taser, so Bartlett went to the ground.

Nieves told Bartlett that Bartlett was going to jail "for harassing my trooper." Nieves then said, "Bet you wish you would have talked to me now."

Bartlett was charged with disorderly conduct and resisting or interfering with an arrest. Those charges were later dismissed by the state.

Bartlett sued under Section 1983, alleging, among other things, excessive force (Fourth Amendment) and freedom of speech (First Amendment) issues.

The federal district court judge ruled that, using the GRAHAM V CONNOR criteria, the officers deserved summary judgment, as they did not exercise excessive force. The court added that if the officers did exercise excessive force, there was no case on point that would have put them on notice that they were violating Bartlett's Fourth Amendment rights, so they deserved qualified immunity.

As to the more interesting issue of the First Amendment violation, the judge ruled that if there were probable cause for the arrest (under Alaska law), it doesn't matter that the officer was retaliating. So the officer was granted summary judgment on this issue.

The Ninth Circuit ruled that the officers deserved summary judgment on the excessive force claim.

However, the court reversed the district court on the retaliatory issue, as there are many cases that hold that arresting someone solely for their speech chills First Amendment rights—even if there were probable cause for the arrest.

The United States Supreme Court took this case for review. The Court ruled that if there is probable cause subjective issues are basically irrelevant. Here there was probable cause. Therefore, the arrest was constitutional.

Ramos v Chicago, 716 F3d 1013 (7th Cir 2013)
An officer is told that a burglary suspect, Jose Ramos, was wearing a red shirt and lived at a certain house. An officer sees a man in a red shirt in a car. The man's name is Pedro Ramos. He is about a foot shorter than the described suspect. The officer handcuffs him.

The Seventh Circuit Court of Appeals, in warning officers about handcuffing with only reasonable suspicion, stated:

> *"Although we have upheld the use of handcuffs to ensure officer safety in a Terry stop of brief duration without automatically escalating the situation to an arrest, that does not mean that law enforcement has a carte blanche to handcuff routinely. The proliferation of cases in this court in which Terry stops involve handcuffs and ever-increasing wait times in police vehicles is disturbing, and we would caution law enforcement officers that the acceptability of handcuffs in some cases does not signal that the restraint is not a significant consideration in determining the nature of the stop."*

Matz v Klatka, 769 F3d517 (2014)
Officers saw a gang member, Salazar, on a porch with a number of other gang members. Salazar was wanted on an armed robbery warrant and was a suspect in homicides and shootings. The officers turned their car around to arrest Salazar and the gang ran. A number of the gang member got into a car. Officers pointed their guns at the gang members and told them to get out of the car, etc. Matz was handcuffed and put in the back seat of the police car. The officers had no probable cause that Matz had done anything wrong. Later Matz confessed to a homicide.

The Seventh Circuit Court of Appeals ruled that the officers deserved summary judgment in this case as they were outnumbered and had to get control of a dangerous situation quickly. The court stated, "The use of a firearm and handcuffs undoubtedly put Matz's encounter at the outer edge of a permissible *Terry* stop...We remind law enforcement that using handcuffs generally signifies an arrest, which requires probable cause...."

Huff v Reichert, 744 F3d 999 (7th Cir, 2014)
Officer Reichert gave Huff's paperwork back after a traffic stop and told him he was free to leave.

After conversing briefly, Reichert asked if he could search Huff's car. Huff replied that he would "just like to go on his way." Reichert told Huff he could leave, but "not in the car." Huff insisted he was being profiled. Reichert searched Huff's car and located "shake." Huff was then allowed to leave.

Huff sued.

The Seventh Circuit Court of Appeals ruled that the officer could not receive qualified immunity stating,

> "A traffic stop can be converted into a full-blown arrest if it extends beyond the time reasonably necessary to complete the purpose for which the stop was made."
>
> *The court also ruled that the case could go to the jury on the "profile" issue too as it was raised during the course of the stop.*

Sornberger v City of Knoxville, 434 F3d 1006 (2006)
Someone robbed a bank. A bank employee who viewed the robbery on video commented that the robber looked a lot like Sornberger, who had previously had an account at the bank. Sornberger was in financial trouble at the time, so he became a prime suspect.

When the employee looked at the video pictures of the robber from a different angle, he noticed there "was less of the likeness." In fact, at certain angles, the robber did not look like Sornberger. The camera footage itself lacked clarity of resolution, so it was hard to make out detail.

An eyewitness to the robbery said the perpetrator was 5'9," about 160 pounds, dark complected, clean shaven, and in his 30s. Sornberger was 5'11," had blond hair, blue eyes, a fair complexion, and a mustache.

Neither the US Attorney nor the state's attorney would authorize an arrest warrant.

The officers picked up both Mr. and Mrs. Sornberger and brought them to the station. Initially both presented identical alibis; they were on the computer at his parents' home. Mrs. Sornberger later confessed to their involvement in the armed robbery. At the suppression hearing, the judge found her confession to be voluntary and in compliance with MIRANDA.

Shortly thereafter a serial armed robber confessed to many robberies, including the one at the bank in question. Officers sent a picture of Sornberger's ear to the FBI to compare it to the bank robber's ear. The FBI concluded that the two ears were different, thereby corroborating the fact that he did not commit the robbery.

The case against the Sornbergers was dismissed, and the Sornbergers sued under Section 1983.

The Federal District Court granted summary judgment in favor of the officers.

The Seventh Circuit ruled that a "reasonable jury certainly could find that probable cause did not exist." Therefore, "a determination of probable cause at the summary judgment stage was improper."

Finally, as to Mrs. Sornberger (Theresa), the Seventh Circuit ruled that the officers who took Theresa to the station could not avail themselves of qualified immunity. Theresa testified that she voluntarily went to the station, but she said that was in response to the officers' statement that she "needed" to accompany them to the station. At the station, she was told that she had been seen at the bank at the time of the robbery (which was a lie), and she was told that her children might be taken from her. So even though she sat in the front seat of the police car and was not handcuffed in any way, the court held that it was a question for the jury as to whether she was restrained in a significant way.

> *The court also ruled that qualified immunity was not available to the officers as the officers misrepresented the facts to the state's attorney when they finally obtained a search warrant for the computer Sornberger was using.*

Buffkins v Omaha, 922 F2d 465 (1990)
An anonymous tipster told police that a black person would be bringing drugs in on a certain plane from Denver. Police observed that there was only one black person on the plane, a female named Buffkins. The officers observed that she appeared nervous and carried a teddy bear that appeared to have been re-sewn.

The officers confronted Buffkins, took her luggage, and escorted Buffkins to the office on the other side of the terminal. At the security office, the officers obtained Buffkins' license and ticket. The officers asked if they could search her bags and Buffkins refused permission. The officers checked out the teddy bear, but determined that it did not contain drugs. Eventually, the officers told Buffkins that she was free to leave. Buffkins responded by calling the officer an "asshole" or said something about the "asshole system." The officers then arrested her for disorderly conduct.

Buffkins sued under Section 1983.

The district court refused to rule that the officers did not have probable cause for the arrest.

But the Court of Appeals ruled that there was no probable cause for the arrest. Therefore, the case was remanded for trial.

Thompson v Wagner, 319 F3d 931 (2003)
Someone bought an expensive diamond at a swap meet. The person paid with a check. The check bounced. The purchaser gave the diamond away, and it was later bartered for a car. The diamond, after passing through many more hands, apparently ended up on the finger of Beverly Thompson. Police traced the diamond to Thompson. The officers spoke to Thompson at her place of work. An officer told Thompson that she had a stolen diamond and that she wouldn't be arrested right then if she admitted guilt and gave it up. Thompson said she was going to call her husband. The officers then put Thompson in handcuffs. The officers testified that they had probable cause to arrest Thompson for obstruction "when she would not permit them to take the ring, and she was going to call her husband and began to walk away."

The district court granted the officers' motion for summary judgment based on qualified immunity.

> *One problem here was that the officers weren't sure that Thompson ended up with the ring and weren't sure that the ring on her finger had the diamond they were looking for. They were sort of guessing.*

The Seventh Circuit Court of Appeals ruled that Thompson could not be guilty of obstruction by simply terminating a voluntary conversation (i.e. there was no probable cause for the arrest). The court also explained that by handcuffing Thompson, the officers could not justify the seizure as a TERRY detention. Finally, the court said the police should have done more investigation before arresting Thompson. Therefore, the district court's holding was reversed and remanded for trial.

Moran v Stratton, 2008 WL 1722148, 2008 U.S. Dist. LEXIS 29537
Moran got a survey to determine the line between her home and the neighbors. The neighbor then put up an orange string, which looked like a surveyor's line, to separate the properties. Unfortunately, the string was on Moran's property. The neighbor then began digging holes on Moran's property to put up a fence and cutting down trees that were on Moran's property. Moran took pictures of all of this.

At some point in this debate, the neighbor called the police. As the police were arriving, Moran was in the process of cutting the string with a pair of scissors. The officer ordered her not to cut the string. Moran asked the officer to take a look at the survey, but the officer refused. The officer then arrested Moran for criminal trespass. Moran alleged she was injured in the arrest and that the officer used excessive force.

The Federal District Court refused to find that the officer deserved qualified immunity.

It is a very bad idea to get in the middle of these disputes. Send them to their attorneys.

Wallace v Chicago, 440 F3d 421 (2006)
Wallace was taken to the Chicago police department on suspicion that he had committed a murder. He confessed.

The Illinois Appellate Court ruled that the officers took Wallace to the station on less than probable cause and questioned him ("Mutt and Jeff" style) until he confessed.

Wallace then sued the officers and the department.

The Seventh Circuit Court of Appeals ruled that Wallace had a cause of action for the illegal/false arrest.

Gauger v Hendle, 349 F3d 354 (2003)
Two elderly people were killed. Officers took their 40-year-old son, Gauger, to the station for questioning for 18 hours. Because there was no forced entry or signs of struggle, the officers thought that Gauger was a prime suspect. Also, Gauger lived with his parents, was an alcoholic, had (allegedly) physically attacked his mother previously, and benefited financially from the death of his parents. The officers obtained a confession from Gauger.

The state then obtained a conviction. Gauger was sentenced to death. Two years later, the Illinois Appellate Court ruled that Gauger's confession was obtained after an unconstitutional seizure (taking the suspect to the station on less than probable cause) and was therefore not admissible. The prosecutor could not re-try Gauger, and he was released from prison.

Gauger then sued under Section 1983 for false arrest.

The Seventh Circuit Court of Appeals ruled that summary judgment/qualified immunity was not available to the detectives and others sued by Gauger.

Fox v Hayes, 600 F3d 819 (7th Cir 2010)
Fox called police because his daughter was missing. She was found soon thereafter in a nearby creek bound, sexually assaulted, and murdered.

Officers asked Fox to come to the station. He did. After he was there and officers accused Fox of murdering his daughter, Fox yelled that he would never do that and tried to leave. The officer said, "Sit your ass down." Fox did so. (This was probably when the jury felt custody/arrest began.) Officers suggested that Fox take a polygraph, and he apparently failed it. Officers then interrogated Fox for several hours and obtained a confession.

Eight months later, the DNA from the sperm was examined and determined not to have come from Fox. The state's attorney dismissed the case and Fox sued under Section 1983.

The state argued that there was probable cause for the arrest for the following undisputed reasons:

- Fox was the last known adult to be with the victim.
- Fox looked for his daughter for 40 minutes before calling police.
- Fox did not call his wife immediately upon determining that the daughter was gone.
- Fox did not reveal that he watched an adult video the night of the murder.
- A vehicle that looked like Fox's was seen at a nearby gas station during the time Fox said he was home. (However, the license number of the vehicle could not be seen.)

Both the jury and the Seventh Circuit Court of Appeals ruled that these facts reflected that Fox was in custody and did not rise to the level of probable cause. The jury awarded Fox $15,500,000. And the Seventh Circuit affirmed the verdict (but reduced the award).

Fittano v Klein, 788 F Supp 1451 (ND IL 1992)
A five-year-old neighbor of Fittano's, Kristina, visited John Fittano's daughter. The next day Kristina told her school teacher that John Fittano had "touched her private parts" in the bathroom of Fittano's home. Kristina also said that Fittano had molested his own daughter. Kristina was interviewed four or five times. During one interview Kristina alleged that there was blood, urine, the devil, death threats, the presence of other men, etc. Each interview contained varied descriptions of what occurred. Based solely on these interviews and the recommendation of the Advocacy Center, an officer arrested Fittano. Fittano consented to the search of his home, but no evidence was found. Later, the grounds for the arrest were determined to be frivolous. (It is hard to determine from the opinion, but apparently during the period when Kristina was at Fittano's home, John Fittano was at a Chicago Bears football game.)

As a result of the arrest, etc., Fittano was deprived of seeing his own daughter for two years and was otherwise deprived of his constitutional rights.

The Seventh Circuit Court of Appeals ruled that the arresting officer could not avail himself of summary judgment or qualified immunity. Furthermore, the court held that the city itself may be liable for "referring investigation of certain classes of criminal activity to an untrained group—the Advocacy Center." The court further stated: "if the Village failed to train its police officers in the proper procedure for handling referrals and arrests in sexual abuse cases, such that its failure to train may be found to amount to deliberate indifference to the plaintiff's rights, the village may be liable under Section 1983." The village's motion to dismiss was therefore also denied.

Beier v Lewiston, 354 P3d 1058 (2003)
Beier (Rafael) and his wife (Susan) were getting divorced. Susan called police when Rafael came to her home. An officer arrived and persuaded Rafael to leave. Susan then got an order of protection. A few days

later, Rafael went to church and sat several rows behind Susan. Susan phoned the officer who had responded before and told him that Rafael was in violation of the protective order. The officer arrived at the church and tried to persuade Rafael to leave. Rafael would not leave stating that he was not in violation of the court order. The officer then arrested Rafael. Rafael would not go peaceably. There was a scuffle, and Rafael subsequently kicked out the window of the police car. The prosecutor dismissed all charges.

Rafael then sued under Section 1983 for false arrest and excessive force.

The Ninth Circuit Court of Appeals ruled that Beier did not violate any term of the protective order. According to the court, the "protection order was available at the church [in Susan's purse]"; the officers should have checked the order themselves. Therefore, the officers could not arrest him. And, therefore, qualified immunity was not available to the officers for the false arrest complaint.

Petersen v Gibson, 372 F2d 862 (2004)
Petersen got her hair colored at a salon. The stylist botched the job twice. On the third try, Petersen was apparently under a hair dryer when her stylist went to lunch and forgot about her. Petersen then left the salon in a huff without paying. The salon called the police. An officer, Gibson, tried to mediate the argument, but Petersen was only willing to pay part of the bill, and the salon would only accept full payment. The officer, therefore, arrested Petersen.

The salon pressed the prosecution for seven months, but finally the state dropped the case.

Petersen sued the salon and the officer and won. Later, the officer settled the suit (for $10,000), and attorneys' fees of $288,087.25 were assessed against Officer Gibson along with court costs.

> *The Seventh Circuit Court of Appeals ruled that if the case is settled, there is no prevailing party, and, therefore, the lower courts' ruling on the attorneys' fees was reversed.*
>
> *Generally, be careful in civil disputes. If possible, lower the emotional level and try to get them to understand that if the "combatants" want a legal answer to settle their dispute, they are going to have to retain a lawyer. If you feel strongly that one of the parties has committed an offense, try to just cite and release the suspect, if possible, and/or explain to the "combatants" that you are going to turn the case over to the state's attorney.*

Williams v Jaglowski, 269 F3d 778 (2001)
Williams was talking to Adams on the phone when she heard a gunshot and then silence. Williams called the police and reported the incident. After the police got to the Adams' residence, Williams showed up. The police began to question Williams, but Williams would not give her date of birth or cooperate. So the police arrested her for obstruction. The case was dropped several weeks later. Williams sued.

The Seventh Circuit Court of Appeals ruled that the officers did not have probable cause to arrest Williams for obstruction simply because she refused to cooperate.

Maxwell v City of Indianapolis, 998 F2d 431 (1993)
Witnesses watched a show on television ("Most Wanted," on criminals) and became convinced that one of their fellow employees was wanted for a crime. The person in question was several inches shorter than the wanted man and almost 100 pounds lighter. Both had grey hair, grey eyes and a missing fingertip (but different fingers). They had similar features and looked similar. Based on the information, the officers arrested the fellow employee.

The Seventh Circuit Court of Appeals ruled that neither summary judgment nor qualified immunity was available to the officers as the dissimilarities (particularly the height and the different finger tips missing) should have alerted the officers to do more investigating before the arrest.

Pourghoraishi v Flying J, 449 F3d 751 (2006)
Pourghoraishi, an Arab truck driver, filled his gas tank and entered the Flying J to pay and to go to the restroom. While waiting to enter the restroom, the manager told Pourghoraishi he could not use the restroom as he had falsified some information related to the obtaining of gas. Since Pourghoraishi had not yet paid for his gas, he said that he would go to the restroom, pay for his gas, and then leave.

An off-duty officer/security guard at the Flying J told Pourghoraishi that he would have to leave. Again Pourghoraishi said he would leave after using the restroom and paying his bill. The officer then allegedly called the Pourghoraishi a "mother f***er" and told him he was going to send him "back to his country." The officer handcuffed Pourghoraishi and searched him finding $160. The officer gave this money to the manager, and the manager gave Pourghoraishi a receipt.

The Seventh Circuit ruled that there were questions of fact as to whether there was probable cause to arrest on disorderly conduct or trespass charges. Therefore, the court held that the case must proceed to trial.

> *One big reason the trespass charge might fail is that the manager said that Pourghoraishi was not going to leave until he paid for his gas. So it is unclear how the truck driver could be trespassing.*

Bibart v Stachowiak, 888 F Supp 864 (ND IL 1995)
An officer stopped Bibart for a traffic offense. There was a warrant out for Bibart's twin sister. The officer arrested Bibart as he didn't believe that Bibart had a twin. The sergeant in charge realized the mistake soon after the arrest and released Bibart (within 30 minutes to three hours of the arrest).

Bibart sued under Section 1983. The Federal District Court ruled that the arresting officer could not seek protection under summary judgment or qualified immunity.

Marshall v Teske, 284 F3d 765 (2002)
Many officers were serving a search warrant in a bad area of the city. A kid, Marshall, saw a bunch of guys (the officers) coming at him with masks on and guns drawn, so he ran. Marshall saw two uniformed officers (who knew nothing about the search warrant execution), and he ran to them for protection. An officer, Teske, serving the warrant, chased Marshall. The two uniformed officers didn't know what was going on until Teske identified himself as an officer. The officers then searched Marshall, even exposing his genitals, but they found no evidence. The officers then arrested Marshall for being a lookout and obstructing.

Marshall received a jury award for compensatory damages and $100,000 in punitive damages against the officers.

The Seventh Circuit ruled that the arrest was clearly without probable cause and was therefore unconstitutional. Therefore, the officers were not entitled to qualified immunity and the jury award was affirmed.

> *The court held that* WARDLOW *did not apply to this situation because the flight was provoked by the officer's conduct. The court, however, conceded that a* TERRY *stop and frisk might have been justified (but probably was not supported by reasonable suspicion).*

Richardson v Bonds, 860 F2d 1427 (1988)
An officer arrested a suspect because the suspect would not give his name.

The Seventh Circuit Court of Appeals ruled that the officer could not gain dismissal by virtue of summary judgment or qualified immunity.

Reher v Vivo, 656 F3d 772 (2011)
Reher was apparently videotaping kids in a park. The police were called out. Sgt. Marilyn Gabinski talked to a witness who also had been the victim of harassment by Reher, about which Gabinski was aware. Gabinski also knew that the victim had filed orders of protection against Reher. When Sgt. Gabinski talked to Reher, he said he was just taping nature. Gabinski told Reher that his story was "bullshit." Reher then said that he didn't want to talk to the "f........ bitch," referring to the sergeant. An officer then arrested Reher for disorderly conduct.

The Seventh Circuit Court of Appeals ruled that calling an officer a name or videotaping in the park is not a crime. Therefore, the arrest was unconstitutional. However, the court ruled that since there was no case right on point, the officer(s) were entitled to qualified immunity.

HUNTER V BRYANT, 502 US 224 (1991)
Bryant wrote a letter that "Mr. Image" was going to kill the president during the President's visit to Germany. A witness also told officers that Bryant had stated that the "President should have been assassinated in Bonn."

Federal officers arrested Bryant, but could not get him to talk about the letter.

The criminal complaint was dismissed. Bryant sued the officers who arrested him without probable cause.

The district court and Court of Appeals held that qualified immunity was not available to the officers because there was no probable cause to believe that Mr. Image was Bryant, and the letter itself does not make a threat against the President.

The United States Supreme Court ruled that the officers deserved to have qualified immunity. Therefore, the Court held that summary judgment should have been awarded the officers.

> *The Court in* BRYANT *reaffirmed a principle first stated in* MALLEY V BRIGGS, 475 US 335 (1985). *The qualified immunity standard "gives ample room for mistaken judgments" by protecting "all but the plainly incompetent or those who knowingly violate the law"* (MALLEY at 343).

Kijonka v Seitzinger, 363 F3d 645 (2004)
Kijonka and Shoulders disliked each other. Kijonka drove by and said to Shoulders, "You have a nice day and your ass is mine, you son of a bitch, and I will get you." Shoulders then said, "Don't you f***in' threaten me!" Officer Seitzinger was standing nearby and later, after consulting with the prosecuting attorney, arrested Kijonka for assault.

The Seventh Circuit Court of Appeals ruled that there was no probable cause for the arrest. The court held, however, that the officer should be granted summary judgment based on qualified immunity since the officer only arrested Kijonka after the prosecutor had told the officer that there was probable cause.

> *This is a good reason to get the okay from a prosecutor before arresting when it is a close case.*

Edwards v Cabrera, 58 F3d 290 (1996)
A bus driver called police stating that he thought he had seen a drug transaction at the Greyhound bus depot. The dispatcher did not give the driver's name. An officer went to the bus station and saw four black men standing together. The group disbanded when they saw the officer. The officer asked one of the men, Edwards, if she (the officer) could speak to him. Edwards agreed and told the officer that he was there simply to drop off his brother. They went to Edwards' brother, who was already on the bus. His brother consented to a search of his luggage, and both Edwards and his brother were arrested. The prosecutor refused to charge Edwards. Edwards sued the police for false imprisonment and the violation of his Fourth Amendment (seizure) rights.

The court ruled that the officers were protected by qualified immunity in that it was not unreasonable for the officers to believe that they had probable cause to arrest Edwards under the circumstances. Therefore, Edwards did not have a viable Section 1983 claim.

Smiddy v Varney, 803 F2d 1469 (1986)
Officers arrested Varney on what they believed was probable cause on a murder charge, as he was the last person seen with the deceased victim. The prosecutor filed a complaint, and the magistrate bound Varney over for trial. Later the case was dismissed for lack of evidence. Varney spent about 30 days in jail.

Varney sued in federal district court under Section 1983. The jury awarded $250,000 for failure to establish probable cause for the arrest.

The Ninth Circuit Court of Appeals ruled that the prosecutor's filing of the case cuts off liability for the officers—unless the officers improperly influenced the prosecutor to file the complaint. Therefore, the case was remanded to see if the officers improperly influenced the prosecutor to file a case in which probable cause did not exist.

Haggerty v Texas Southern University, 391 F3d 653 (2004)
Haggerty, a teacher at Texas Southern University (TSU), saw that about eight students were beating up a student named Randolph. Haggerty called TSU officers. An officer handcuffed Randolph as he was "out of control." Haggerty told the officers not to handcuff Randolph. Officers told Haggerty to back off, or he would be arrested. Shortly thereafter, Randolph apparently tried to break free and attack the students, so the officer slammed Randolph against a wall. Haggerty again attempted to intervene. Walking toward the officer from about 10 to 15 feet away, he told the officer not to "manhandle that juvenile." The officers then arrested Haggerty for interference with the duties of a public servant.

The trial court held that the officer should have known that a person (Haggerty) cannot be arrested when the "interference" consists of "speech only." Therefore, the court denied the motion to grant the officer qualified immunity.

The Fifth Circuit Court of Appeals reversed, ruling that a reasonable officer could have mistakenly believed that there was probable cause to arrest, especially because Haggerty was approaching the officer as he spoke and because the officers had not yet gotten control of the scene. Therefore, the court ruled that qualified immunity was appropriate in this case.

> *Always be careful about arresting someone for talking. Remember the First Amendment guarantees freedom of speech.*

Lauer v Dahlberg, 717 F Supp 612 (ND IL 1989)
An officer arrested Lauer based on an arrest warrant. Lauer presented the officer with a copy of the recall order, but it was not certified by the clerk. The officer re-checked through LEADS and Central Dispatch to

make sure the warrant was still active. Apparently the warrant had been re-called the day before, but this information had not yet been disseminated.

Lauer sued. The Seventh Circuit Court of Appeals ruled that it was not unreasonable for Dahlberg to believe that the warrant was good. Therefore, qualified immunity was appropriate.

White v Olig, 56 F3d 817 (1995)
An officer stopped a car on a traffic offense (the car in which Willie White was riding). After checking, the officer determined that there was a Willie White with the same birth date who had a court order for a body attachment. Many other parts of the description, however, were incorrect including the fact that White was described as being white, while the person in the vehicle was black. The officer asked White about the attachment, and White said that he thought he had taken care of that. The officer then took White into custody. The body attachment turned out to be for a different Willie White.

White sued.

The district court and Seventh Circuit Court of Appeals granted summary judgment/qualified immunity for the officer.

Excessive/unreasonable force cases

Excessive force cases almost always arise under the Tier 2 (TERRY stops) or Tier 3 (custody) model discussed at length in Chapter 2 (on the search and seizure of persons).

An important fact that every officer needs to know is that if you stand around and watch an officer exercise excessive force, you are just as liable as the officer exercising the excessive force. See Lewis v Downey, 581 F3d 767 (7th Cir 2009).

The factors of excessive force: deadly and non-deadly force

There is really only one factor related to when an officer may exercise deadly force; that is, did the person against whom the officer exercised deadly force represent a threat of deadly force or serious bodily injury to the officer or other person. Tennessee v Garner, 471 US 1 (1985)

The most important case in the history of excessive/unreasonable non-deadly force law is GRAHAM V CONNOR [490 US 386 (1989)].

The United States Supreme Court in GRAHAM gave guidance as to three factors that should be assessed in every excessive force case:

- The severity of the crime
- Whether the person against whom the force was used presented an immediate threat
- Whether the person against whom the force was used was resisting arrest or trying to escape

These factors are not the only factors (e.g. warning the suspect and whether the suspect is being detained or is under arrest are also very important) and need not be recited verbatim as jury instructions. [Fikes v Cleghorn, 47 F3d C 1011 (1995)].

Use of force that is greater than might be used

The normal rule is that an officer need not use the least force or all feasible alternatives; the rule is that officers must use <u>reasonable</u> force. This is especially the case when officers use deadly force when confronted with someone who represents a threat of serious bodily injury or death.

Plakas v Drinski, 19 F3d 1143 (1994)
Plakas was drunk and drove his car into a ditch. An officer found Plakas walking along the road. Plakas admitted to driving the car in the ditch. The officer arrested Plakas but Plakas escaped. Plakas fled to his fiancé's home which was nearby. Officers followed Plakas to the home. Plakas grabbed a fireplace poker and hit one of the officers on his wrist. Plakas then took off out the door. The officers surrounded him. At one point Plakas said to one officer that one of them was going to die. After a 15-minute interval where the officers tried to calm Plakas and get him to drop the poker, Plakas began to approach an officer with the poker raised. The officer shot and killed Plakas.

Plakas' executor sued the officers, arguing that the officers had the duty to use all less deadly force or alternative methods (including pepper spray) to resolve the situation before using deadly force.

The Seventh Circuit Court of Appeals ruled that the force used was reasonable under the circumstances and that the officers were not required here to use their pepper spray or lesser degrees of force. Therefore, summary judgment was appropriate.

> *Many state legislatures, including Illinois, are trying to create a statute that prohibits the use of deadly force unless it is "necessary." This will make it even more difficult for officers under great stress to determine when they can use deadly force and when they cannot.*

Pena v Leombruni, 200 F3d 1031 (1999)
A man shoplifted and acted crazy in a store. An officer arrived and could see the man, Pena, was mentally unstable. When Pena confronted the officer, the officer felt compelled to pepper spray the man and his dog. Pena then picked up a chunk of concrete. The officer back-pedaled and told the man to put the concrete down. When Pena was within five to ten feet, the officer shot Pena and killed him.

Pena's administrator sued the officer for excessive force, arguing that the officer should have been trained to handle mentally ill or unstable people without shooting them.

The Seventh Circuit Court of Appeals ruled that the officer may respond with deadly force if the officer reasonably believes that he is in imminent danger of great bodily injury or death. Therefore, summary judgment was appropriate.

Sherrod v Berry, 856 F2d 802 (1988)
An officer, Berry, heard a police radio broadcast that a certain store had been "robbed." The officer saw the offenders in a parking lot and told them to raise their hands. The driver, Sherrod, dropped his arm suddenly, and Berry shot and killed him. There was no gun in Sherrod's car.

Unfortunately, the clerk at the store had apparently not been "robbed"—there was simply a theft from the store, but there was no gun used. The clerk had called it in as a robbery as the clerk did not know the difference.

Officer Berry and the city were sued under Section 1983 alleging excessive force.

At the jury trial, the jury awarded $1,000,000. One reason for this was that the jury was informed that there was a material fact related to Sherrod's having no gun—rather different than the question of whether the officer reasonably believed that Sherrod had a gun.

The Seventh Circuit Court of Appeals ruled that the real issue was whether the officer reasonably believed that his life was in danger based only on what Sherrod did—not that Sherrod had no gun. To allow a jury to determine liability of the officer based on information the officer did not have is unfair to the officer. Therefore, the judgment at the trial court level was reversed and the case remanded for a new trial.

The point here is that if there were "facts" that led an officer to reasonably believe he/she needed to use a particular level of force, the fact that the officer was wrong is irrelevant. This doesn't mean that officers cannot be impeached/cross examined if the officer says he/she saw something shiny in a suspect's hand, but the suspect is shown later to have nothing shiny.

Carlson v Bukovic, 621 F3d 610 (7th Cir 2010)
A man and his mother were arguing with WalMart personnel when the police were called. When the mother, who was 83 years old, began arguing with the officer and becoming loud, the store personnel asked her to leave. The officer escorted the lady out of the store physically. The lady argued that the officer used excessive force in the removal.

The Seventh Circuit Court of Appeals ruled that the officer could not avail himself of qualified immunity and that it was a question for the jury as to whether the plaintiff was free to leave or ignore the officer.

Why courts do not award summary judgment and instead give excessive force cases to a jury.
"Unreasonable force claims are generally fact questions for the jury" [Hervey v Estes, 65 F3d 784 (1995)]. The reason is obvious—the defendant is hurt and he normally will tell a different story than the officer(s) does (do) about how he got hurt. As long as there is a material fact which the parties disagree on (e.g. how much force was used), only the jury can decide the case. This is a bad fact of life for officers.

Pre-seizure tactics and conduct
Plaintiffs suing officers often argue that, if the officer(s) had executed better pre-seizure tactics or strategy, there would have been no need for the amount of force exerted against the citizen/suspect. At times, the Seventh Circuit has apparently bought into this idea.

Estate of Starks v Enyart, 5 F3d 230 (7th Cir 1993)
Starks stole a taxi cab. He parked in a Taco Bell parking lot. Three officers approached Starks. According to an independent eye witness, Starks attempted to drive off going forward. He had a very narrow path to escape beside a utility pole. An officer jumped out from behind the utility pole and shot Starks. The other officers shot Starks too.

The Federal District ruled that the officers should get summary judgment as Starks represented a threat of serious bodily injury or death, so deadly force was justified.

The Seventh Circuit ruled that the officer put himself in harm's way and, therefore, did not deserve summary judgment.

Deadly force
The reasonability of seizures (and using the Fourth Amendment to determine reasonability) began with the landmark case of TENNESSEE V GARNER, where the Supreme Court discussed the reasonability of shooting a fleeing felon. The Court, in holding that such shootings must be "reasonable," also held that these "seizures" must be analyzed under Fourth Amendment doctrine and that shooting someone is a seizure.

The rule for deadly force is that deadly force is reasonable if the person against whom the deadly force is "executed" represents an **imminent threat of death or serious bodily injury**.

TENNESSEE V GARNER, 471 US 1 (1985)
Officers received a radio message that a certain home was being burglarized. They went to the home and saw a boy or young man, Garner, running from the home. An officer told Garner to stop, but Garner kept fleeing. When it became apparent that Garner was going to escape, the officer shot and killed Garner.

The United States Supreme Court ruled that the officer's shooting Garner was a seizure under the Fourth Amendment and that the seizure was unreasonable because Garner did not pose a threat to anyone at the time he was shot.

> GARNER *was the landmark case where the Supreme Court said that seizures for purposes of civil liability must be tested under the Fourth Amendment standard. That is, was the seizure "reasonable"?*
>
> *"Deadly force is force that creates a substantial risk of causing death or serious bodily harm." This can be a gun or even a dog trained to go for the jugular* [e.g. Chew v Gates, 27 F3d 1432 (1994)].

WHITE V PAULY, 137 US 548 (2017)
Dan Pauly was involved in a road rage situation. Two women who were the victims of road rage followed him to his home. Officers arrived and ordered Pauly to open the door and come out. Pauly did not respond. Pauly and his brother got guns and told officers they had guns. Officer White came onto the scene late and did not know what had transpired. Both brothers fired their guns. White shot and killed Dan's brother. Dan Pauly sued and later said that he did not know that it was police officers knocking on the door.

The Tenth Circuit ruled that White gave no warning. Therefore, White did not deserve qualified immunity, and a jury could find him liable.

The United States Supreme Court reversed ruling that White deserved qualified immunity as there was no case on point that would have told him that he was violating the Constitution when he shot Pauly.

> *The United States Supreme Court is constantly reversing the circuit courts and holding that the officer deserves qualified immunity in these deadly force cases. The problem is that the Supreme Court refuses to say whether the officers' conduct was constitutional or unconstitutional. To be safe, officers should assume the officer's conduct in cases like White was unconstitutional when the courts only decide the officers deserve qualified immunity. The real tip in White is to give a warning before you shoot—if you can.*

Brown v Blanchard, 31 F Supp 3d 1003 (7th Cir 2016)
Brown had told people he was thinking of committing suicide, had locked himself in the bedroom, and had a knife nearby. Brown was bipolar and had not taken his medication. He also had drunk a lot of alcohol.

- Nancy Brown, his mother, had previously entered the room and hugged Brown and talked to him.
- The officers did not first attempt to use less than deadly force.

- The officers could see Brown through a window and could see that Brown was not hurting himself—but that he had a knife and alcohol nearby.
- The officers broke in the door and shot Brown.
- Nancy Brown did not hear the officers give any commands to Brown before shooting him.

The Seventh Circuit Court of Appeals ruled that the officers here did not deserve qualified immunity as there was a "material" question of facts (which only a jury can resolve) in that Brown's mother said the officers did not tell Brown to drop the knife. Also, Brown's mother testified that Brown was not aggressive and that she had previously held her son's head. So the court basically held that a jury might rule that Brown did not charge the officers with a knife.

Summary Judgment—No Constitutional Violation

The following are cases where the courts held that the person against whom the officers exercised deadly force represented a threat of death or serious bodily injury.

WHITE V PAULY, 137 US 548 (2017)

Dan Pauly was apparently involved in a road rage incident. Two women, who were apparent victims of the road rage, told police that Pauly was drunk, "swerving all crazy" at night in the rain. The women talked to Pauly, and after that brief nonviolent encounter, Pauly drove to his home where he lived with his brother Samuel. The women gave an officer Pauly's license number.

Officer(s) went to Pauly's home and yelled for Pauly to "open the door." The Paulys testified that they did not hear the officers identify themselves—only that they were "coming in."

Samuel got a handgun and Daniel got a shotgun. The Pauly brothers then told the officers that they had guns. White came onto the scene late and hid behind a stone wall. He missed what had happened previously.

Both of the brothers fired their guns while screaming loudly. Samuel pointed his gun in White's direction and fired it. White then shot and killed Samuel.

The Tenth Circuit Court of Appeals ruled that a jury could consider Officer White's conduct to be unreasonable under the circumstances mainly because White gave no warning. The court, therefore, refused to grant White qualified immunity.

This per curiam opinion reversed the Tenth Circuit, stating that Officer White deserved qualified immunity as there was no case on point that would have put Officer White on notice that under these circumstances he must give a warning.

PLUMHOFF V RICKARD, 134 S Ct 2012 (2014)

An officer pulled Rickard's car over because it had only one operating headlight. Rickard did not have a license and was acting very nervous, so the officer told Rickard to step out of the car. Rickard then drove off.

Officers (five cars) chased Rickard as Rickard drove at speeds over 100 mph, passing dozens of cars. Rickard exited the highway, collided with Plumhoff's car and was soon cornered. However, Rickard managed to extract himself. During this period, Plumhoff and other officers got out of their cars. Plumhoff fired three shots into Rickard's car. Rickard sped off. Officers then fired 12 more shots. Rickard and his passenger were hit with the bullets. Rickard drove the car into a building. Both Rickard and his passenger died from some combination of gunshot wounds and injuries caused by the crash.

Rickard's daughter filed a Section 1983 action.

The Federal District Court and the Federal Court of Appeals ruled that the officers did not deserve summary judgment.

The United States Supreme Court ruled that this case was just like SCOTT V HARRIS (below)—a high-speed chase where the driver represented a threat of serious bodily injury or death to the others on the road. Therefore, the officers did not violate Rickard's rights by using deadly force to stop him.

As a backup ruling, the Court also ruled that the officers deserved qualified immunity as the facts in this case are better for the officers than the ones in BROSSEAU V HAUGEN (below). In that case Haugen had not already endangered lives. Rickard clearly HAD already endangered a lot of lives with his reckless driving.

> *There is a possibility that the (estates of the) occupants of the vehicle (particularly the passenger) could have won their case had they brought the suit as a common law tort, where the test for liability is "wanton and willful" (in Illinois), as in that circumstance the departmental rules would in all likelihood be admissible, and most departments forbid shooting at a driver in this situation.*

SCOTT V HARRIS, 127 S Ct 1209 (2007)
Deputy Scott chased Harris at speeds nearing 90 mph. Scott then intentionally bumped Harris' vehicle, causing the vehicle to spin out of control. As a result, Harris' vehicle crashed and Harris was rendered quadriplegic. Harris sued under Section 1983.

The United States Supreme Court ruled that the officer's bumping Harris' vehicle was a seizure. The Court further held that the seizure was deadly force applied constitutionally/reasonably because Harris posed a substantial immediate risk of serious bodily injury to others.

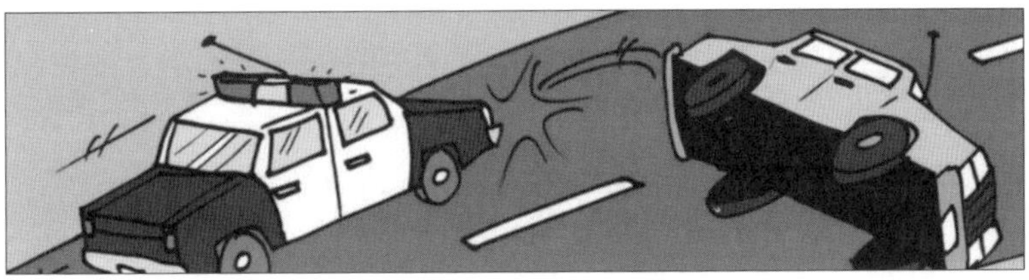

Officers may well lose this case under common law where the standard is wanton and willful.

Common v City of Chicago, 661 F3d 940 (2011)
A store owner told officers that a certain robbery suspect often entered the store, but by the time police got to the store the suspect was gone. An officer gave the store owner his cell phone and told the store owner to call him if the suspect returned. The officer received a call from the store owner and immediately responded to the store. The suspect, Smith, and two others were just leaving the store. The officer told the suspects to show their hands. The two others showed their hands. Smith did not. The officer started to take out his gun, but Smith grabbed for the officer's wrist. The officer pulled the gun and shot Smith. Later it was determined that Smith had drugs in his mouth – but did not have drugs in his system.

The Seventh Circuit Court of Appeals ruled that the drugs were admissible to prove that Smith would act as he did in order to keep the officer from discovering the drugs.

Sanzone v Gray, 884 F3d 734 (7th Cir 2018)
Officers were called to the home of Koster as he was having trouble breathing. Emergency personnel told Koster they were present to help him. Koster yelled, "If you enter my apartment, I will shoot you!" The SWAT team showed up, and Koster pulled a gun and pointed it. Officers then shot Koster.

The Seventh Circuit Court of Appeals ruled that because it was undisputed that Koster pointed a gun at the officers, the officers' use of deadly force was constitutional.

Palmquist v Selvik, 111 F3d 1332 (7th Cir 1997)
Officers were dispatched to a call that a man, Palmquist, was screaming obscenities, making death threats, howling at the moon and breaking windows. When officers arrived, they attempted to calm Palmquist, but matters soon got out of hand when Palmquist hit an officer with a muffler pipe. An officer then shot and maimed Palmquist, but Palmquist then said, "You only winged me—you'll have to kill me." The officers ended up killing Palmquist.

At trial the officers tried to introduce evidence that Palmquist had told others that he wanted to commit "suicide by cop."

The Seventh Circuit Court of Appeals ruled that this evidence was not admissible because the officers were not aware of the fact that Palmquist had made this statement nor was it admissible that Palmquist was drunk as the officers were apparently unaware of this fact also.

Forrett v Richardson, 112 F3d 416 (1997)
Forrett bound and shot two victims during a burglary. He then stole firearms and a truck. A victim called the police and described the crimes and the truck. The officers found the truck abandoned. A few minutes later they saw a man matching Forrett's description. An officer confronted Forrett, and Forrett fled on foot.

Forrett eluded the officers for about an hour as he ran through the neighborhood. Officers told residents in the neighborhood to stay indoors as they thought Forrett would take hostages if he could. Officers saw him again and ordered him to surrender. Forrett ran, so the officers shot and wounded him.

Forrett sued the officers, the chief, and the city. Forrett argued that he was not armed and, therefore, did not pose a threat to the officers or others.

A jury awarded compensatory and punitive damages against the defendants, even though Forrett admitted that there was probable cause to arrest for the offenses.

The Ninth Circuit Court of Appeals ruled that the officers had probable cause to believe that Forrett would use violent means to escape if he had to, including the seizing of a hostage, if he were not apprehended. The court also ruled that it was reasonable to use deadly force in such circumstances. Therefore, the officers did not violate Forrett's constitutional rights.

Scott v Edinburg, 346 F3d 752 (2003)
An officer, Edinburg, was off duty and drove his car to a hot dog stand. He parked at a gas station next to the stand. He left his keys in the car. Scott got in the car and started to drive it away. Edinburg told Scott that the car was his and to stop. The car's reverse lights came on, and the car backed up toward Edinburg. Officer Edinburg moved aside and yelled, "Stop! Police!" and drew his revolver. As the car then sped forward, the officer fired shots. Scott drove away at a high rate of speed. The officer followed on foot into the street and fired several more bullets. One of the bullets killed Scott.

The parties agreed that Scott died from one of the "first few shots fired by Officer Edinburg, while he was on the gas station property." The parties also agreed that there were 12 to 14 pedestrians in the gas station parking lot. Two witnesses swore under oath that no one was in the direct path of the car and that no one was forced to move away as the car sped off. Edinburg stated that two people were in the path and that others were running away.

Edinburg's instructor "testified that shooting into a moving vehicle and the use of deadly force against a non-dangerous fleeing felon is a violation of police procedures."

The Seventh Circuit Court of Appeals ruled that summary judgment was properly granted for the defendant officers.

> *The court further determined that the issue is not one of violation of department policies but whether Edinburg violated the constitutional rights of Scott. Therefore, whether Edinburg violated departmental rules is usually irrelevant to a Section 1983 action.*

Qualified Immunity—No case law/doctrine to put officer on notice

The following are cases where the courts ruled that the case must be dismissed against the officer because there was no doctrine/case law in place putting the officer on notice that deadly force would be excessive in the situation. (See also PLUMHOFF V RICKARD, above.)

SAN FRANCISCO V SHEEHAN, 135 S Ct 1765 (2015)

Sheehan lived in a room in a facility for people with mental illnesses. A social worker stopped in to see Sheehan in her room, as Sheehan had stopped taking her medication and was no longer changing her clothes or eating. Sheehan told the social worker that she had a knife and would kill him if he didn't leave.

The social worker left and called the police. The social worker then sought—and received—help to get Sheehan to a hospital for treatment as she was obviously a danger to other people.

An officer arrived but realized quickly that she needed backup and called her sergeant. The two of them entered Sheehan's room after knocking and announcing their purpose. They told her when they knocked that they wanted to help her. Sheehan grabbed a 5-inch kitchen knife and told the officers that she was going to kill them. The officers retreated out of the room, and Sheehan closed the door.

The officers heard sirens, indicating more backup was on the way. The officers decided to immediately re-enter and subdue Sheehan before backup arrived. The officers entered Sheehan's room with pistols drawn. The sergeant immediately pepper sprayed Sheehan. When Sheehan attacked the officers with a knife, the officers shot her.

The prosecutor could not get a conviction against Sheehan, and Sheehan sued under Section 1983 for entering her room without a warrant and excessive force.

The Federal District Court ruled that the officers should be accorded summary judgment on the exigency issue because they had to act quickly in that they didn't know if:

- Sheehan would go out the back window (although she was on the second floor) or
- Whether there was someone else in Sheehan's room whom Sheehan might harm or
- Whether she might hurt herself.

The Ninth Circuit Court of Appeals reversed ruling that there was "no objective need for immediate entry." The Ninth Circuit decided that the officers "provoked" the response from Sheehan, and, therefore, the case must go to a jury.

The United States Supreme Court basically agreed with the District Court on the facts supporting the emergency entry; but ruling that, even if the officers were wrong, they deserved qualified immunity, concluding that everyone has 20/20 hindsight and that it's easy to second guess officers in this very tense circumstance.

KISELA V HUGHES, 138 S Ct 1148 (2018)
A neighbor called and told police that a woman was hacking at a tree with a kitchen knife and otherwise acting erratically. Officers arrived and confirmed the story of the neighbor. They then saw Hughes, the woman with a knife, apparently confronting another woman. The police all yelled for Hughes to put the knife down. Hughes acted as if she didn't hear the officers. The woman that Hughes was confronting told the police to "take it easy." Officer Kisela shot Hughes four times. The two other officers did not fire as they felt they wanted to continue to try verbal commands.

The court of appeals ruled that Kisela did not deserve qualified immunity as there were many cases that put the officer on notice that he should not shoot someone in this situation.

The United States Supreme Court apparently felt that Kisela violated Hughes' rights, but since there was no case right on point that would have put Kisela on notice, the Court ruled that Kisela deserved qualified immunity.

MULLENIX V LUNA, 136 S Ct 305, 193 L Ed 2d 255 (2015)
An officer had a misdemeanor arrest warrant for the suspect. The officer saw the suspect at a fast food restaurant. When the officer told the suspect he was under arrest, the suspect drove off. Officers chased the suspect at speeds allegedly between 85 and 110 mph. The suspect twice called dispatch threatening to shoot at police if they did not cut off their pursuit.

Officers set up three sets of spike strips. About 20 minutes after the pursuit began, Officer Mullenix, standing in an overpass directly over the spike strips, contacted his superior asking about whether he could shoot at the suspect's engine block of the car. His supervisor said to stand by and see if the spikes worked first. Mullenix shot six times at the car when the car was 25-30 yards from the spike sticks, hitting the suspect four times and killing him. After the suspect's car hit the spike sticks, it rolled two and a half times.

The suspect's estate sued under Section 1983 alleging that Officer Mullenix violated the suspect's Fourth Amendment rights by shooting into the car—seizing him with a bullet—in law enforcement terminology, exercising excessive force.

The federal district court ruled that there were "genuine issues of fact as to whether Trooper Mullenix" violated the suspect's rights and that there were cases on point that put Mullenix on notice that he was violating the suspect's rights. Therefore, Mullenix was not in position to even avail himself of qualified immunity.

The Federal Court of Appeals affirmed stating that a jury could find that the officer should not have shot the suspect under the circumstance. The court reasoned that there were three big differences between this case and the United States Supreme Court cases where the officers were awarded summary judgment because they did not violate the suspect's rights:

- There were no innocent bystanders in this case;
- The suspect's driving was relatively controlled;
- There were spike strips that would have stopped the suspect's car.

The United States Supreme Court ruled that Officer Mullenix deserved qualified immunity as the facts of no case previously decided would have put the officer on notice that his conduct was unconstitutional.

Factually, the suspect had already said twice he was going to kill officers if they did not break off the chase. And he was about to encounter an officer stationed moments away. The Court also noted that spike strips do not always work. Therefore, the suspect represented a threat of serious bodily injury or death.

Estate of Williams v The Indiana State Police Department, 797 F3d 468 (7th Cir 2015)
Family members called police to their home because Williams had threatened to commit suicide and had locked himself in the bathroom. Williams had already cut himself and said that it was taking too long to bleed out. He had taken a number of Xanax pills, and he threatened to kill anyone who came into the bathroom. The officers unlocked the door and tried to subdue Williams with a taser. The taser didn't work. Williams then attacked the officers with a knife. The officers shot and killed Williams.

The Seventh Circuit Court of Appeals ruled that the officers in this case deserved qualified immunity as there was no case at the time that would have put the officers on notice that their conduct was unconstitutional.

BROSSEAU V HAUGEN, 543 US 194 (2004)
Officers had a felony no-bail warrant on Haugen for drugs and "other offenses." An officer saw Haugen running for his jeep. The officer pulled her handgun and ordered him to stop. The officer hit the driver's side window with her gun and broke the window. Haugen began to drive away. The officer shot Haugen in the back.

The officer later told department investigators that she thought Haugen had committed burglaries and that she did not fear for her safety. She did not see a weapon in Haugen's hand but only keys, as he was trying to start the truck. The officer stated further that she thought if Haugen had a gun, he might use it on her fellow officers or that he might run the truck into them.

The following is a short salient portion of her interview:

Q: At that point, who then did you become concerned about?
A: My concern at that point and time were for the vehicles directly in front of him, one... which [was] occupied by a woman and her child. And the other officers that I felt were in the immediate area—that were coming on foot to back me up. I was quite sure that some of them were right close to where he was driving.
Q: How close do you think his speeding car came from striking [the car with the woman and the child]?
A: I don't know.
Q: Okay. Was it within ten feet?
A: I don't know... I'm having some trouble with perceptions of distances.
Q: Okay. Can you estimate how close you were to his car when you fired the shot?
A: No. Not at this time...
Q: Okay. And once again, just so that I know for sure, can you give me your basis for the reasonable belief that other people's lives were threatened?
A: First of all, I still had in mind that he had a weapon. I thought that it would be very difficult for him to try and shoot at me from the position we were at when I fired. However, I felt that he could have fired on any officers in front of him or the people in the pickup truck, who he had cause to be unhappy with. And his driving more than anything else. His vehicle. I did not believe he could see where he was going. He was driving in an erratic manner. Now we had pedestrians and officers and residents in the area.

The trial court found that Haugen had no gun, and the officer shot Haugen before he even started to drive off or was, at worst, just starting to drive off. Next, she didn't know where her fellow officers were. Finally, she shot Haugen with civilians in the possible line of fire.

The Ninth Circuit Court of Appeals ruled that an officer may not use deadly force to arrest a fleeing suspect unless the suspect poses an immediate, serious threat to the officer or others. The court said the threat here was mere speculation. Therefore, qualified immunity was not available to the officer.

The United States Supreme Court reversed the Ninth Circuit, holding that there was no case on point (including TENNESSEE V GARNER) that would guide the officer that her conduct at the time was unconstitutional. Therefore, the officer/defendant was entitled to qualified immunity.

Gant v Hartman, 924 F3d 445 (2019
Officers were dispatched to the armed robbery of employees of a Dollar General store. Officer Hartman and several other officers took a position near the front door. A couple of officers in the back radioed that the robbers tried to get out the back but decided to go back in toward the front. One robber started to run away, and officers chased him. As that occurred, Gant held the door open. Officer Hartman shot him in the stomach. The officer was within about 20 feet of Gant when the officer shot Gant. Hartman said he believed Gant was holding a gun, but Gant was not. Gant said he was trying to surrender. This scene was videotaped.

Gant pled guilty to the crime of armed robbery and sued Hartman under Section 1983 for violation of his Fourth Amendment rights.

The district court judge ruled that the officer did not deserve qualified immunity, as a jury, basing their decision on the facts, could decide that Gant was in the process of obeying commands or did not have the opportunity to obey Hartman's commands.

The Seventh Circuit also ruled that the officer did not deserve qualified immunity.

Constitutional Violation – No Qualified Immunity
The following are cases where the courts ruled that summary judgment/qualified immunity was not appropriate and the defendant(s) were required to go to trial or settle the case.

Estate of Starks v Enyart, 5 F3d 230 (7th Cir 1993)
Starks stole a taxi cab. He parked in a Taco Bell parking lot. Three officers approached Starks. According to an independent eye witness, Starks attempted to drive off going forward. He had a very narrow path to escape beside a utility pole. An officer jumped out from behind the utility pole and shot Starks. The other officers shot Starks too.

The Federal District ruled that the officers should get summary judgment as Starks represented a threat of serious bodily injury.

The Seventh Circuit ruled that the officer put himself in harm's way and, therefore, did not deserve summary judgment.

Harris v Roderick, 126 F2d 1189 (1997)
Officers went to serve an arrest warrant on a man, Randy Weaver, in his cabin/home. The officers got into a gun battle with a couple of people in a house. One officer was killed and one person from the house was killed. The officers were then told by supervisory order to shoot any adult male with a weapon in the vicinity of the house. A sharpshooter shot a male, Harris, who had left the house with a gun and was running, trying to get back into the cabin.

Harris sued for violation of his Fourth Amendment rights. He said that there was no probable cause that he had done anything wrong. And the officers had no reason to believe that he was an immediate threat to anyone. Finally, he argued that the officers never warned him before shooting him.

The Ninth Circuit Court of Appeals ruled that qualified immunity was not available for the sharpshooter. According to the court, Harris was not escaping, simply retreating into the cabin. There was absolutely no imminent danger of death or serious bodily injury. Therefore, deadly force could not be used.

Non-deadly force

When an officer is sued for using too much force during a stop or arrest, the test the court will use is the Fourth Amendment. The test for excessive force was laid down in GRAHAM V CONNOR:

- What was the crime? Was it serious?
- What was the threat to the officer?
- What was the resistance?

These factors are not "exclusive" (i.e. the Supreme Court stated that lower courts may create others. See below). For example, a court may consider whether an officer gave warnings and whether the suspect was being detained or under arrest.

GRAHAM V CONNOR, 490 US 386 (1989)

Graham was suffering from an insulin problem and was driven to a convenience store by a friend to purchase orange juice. Graham ran into the store; but when he realized that the line was too long, he ran out and got into the car. Officers watching the store saw Graham run into the convenience store and quickly run out, so the officers thought that he had just committed a robbery. The officers then stopped the car. Graham ran around the car and sat on the curb. The officers thought Graham was on drugs, so an officer banged his face on the hood of the car (presumably to clear his head). An officer then checked the convenience store and learned that Graham did not rob the store.

The United States Supreme Court ruled that the suit must be analyzed under the Fourth Amendment. That is, was the seizure "unreasonable?" (Obviously, even if the officers had reasonable suspicion to stop, they did not have the power during the detention to bash his face on the hood of the car.)

Since GRAHAM, the Seventh Circuit has been willing to look at other factors, while at least giving lip service to the fact that the GRAHAM factors are the most important:

- Did the officer give a warning?
- Was the officer engaged in a detention/traffic or an arrest situation?
- Was there a big size difference?

The courts basically set a pyramid of force below that of deadly force:

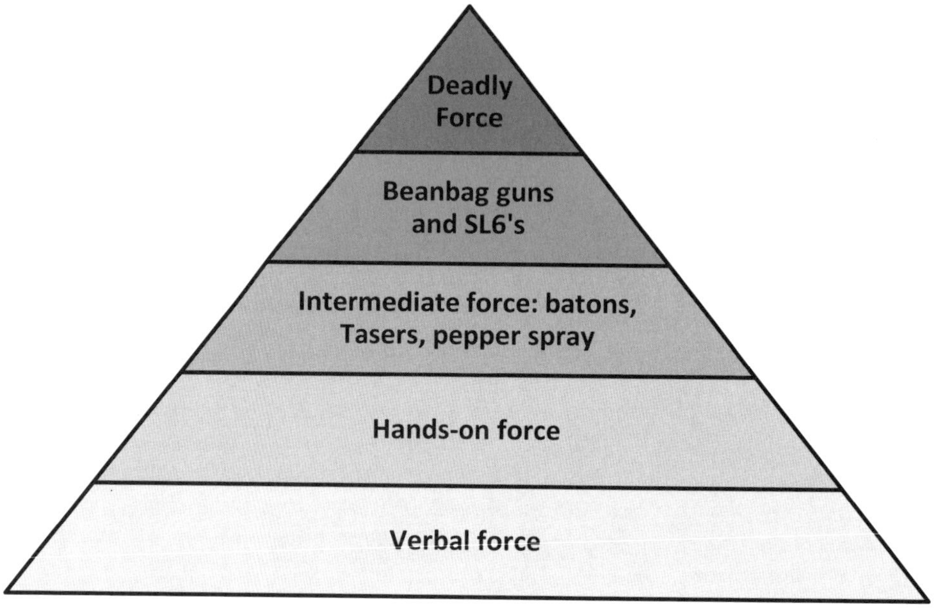

Beanbag guns, SL6's, and similar type "guns"

Beanbag guns and other like weapons (such as the SL6) have generally been treated as less than deadly force but more than intermediate force (like batons, Tasers, and pepper spray) and so must be used with great circumspection. At close range, most courts say that these weapons can constitute deadly force.

Bell v Irwin, 321 F3d 637 (2003)

Bell got drunk and threatened his wife. Mrs. Bell called the police. By the time the police arrived, the couple had made up and asked the police to leave them alone. Within an hour, the couple got into another fight, and Mrs. Bell was knocking on doors seeking protection from her husband. Bell had torn up the couple's home. The officers initiated a background check of Bell and learned that Bell had a history of arrests for domestic violence, unlawful use of weapons, obstruction of justice, and drunk driving.

Bell had a number of knives and a meat cleaver. Bell threw a number of the knives in the yard. He held a knife to his throat telling the officers that he would kill himself. He told officers that he would kill any officer who came in after him. He further said that he would only come out "feet first."

The officers called out a negotiator, who was unsuccessful. Bell opened the door and threatened to blow up his home using the propane and kerosene in tanks outside. An officer with a beanbag gun shot Bell as Bell approached the tank with what appeared to be a lighter. It took four rounds to bring him down—one round hit him in the head.

Bell and his wife sued for excessive force under Section 1983.

The trial court found that the beanbag gun constituted deadly force (but less lethal than bullets or buckshot). (The case does not state how far the officer was from Bell when he fired the shots.) The defendants apparently acquiesced in the notion that beanbags are "a species of deadly force." Nevertheless, the court awarded summary judgment in favor of the defendants.

The Bells argued that the only ones who should determine whether the police should have used other—less deadly—methods is a jury.

The Seventh Circuit Court of Appeals ruled that the officers' conduct was reasonable, stating: "We think that Bell should have thanked rather than sued the officers. True, he suffered injury at their hands, but in his depressed and irrational state aggravated by liquor, he might have done himself or others greater injury had they not intervened." The court held, therefore, that summary judgment in favor of the defendants/officers was appropriate.

> *This would appear to be a highly threatening situation justifying the use of a beanbag gun. See the next case, Phillips, for an opposite result.*

Phillips v Community Insurance Corporation, 678 F3d 513 (7th Cir 2012)

Officers received a dispatch that the driver of a vehicle with stolen plates was driving recklessly and might be drunk.

The driver apparently drove onto the driveway of an apartment complex, but the car was facing out toward the street and the driver had backed into a hedgerow. The lights were on, and the officers assumed the ignition was activated. Police cars apparently formed sort of a semi-circle around the front of the suspect car, sort of hemming the suspect vehicle in. The officers pointed their spotlights on the driver, who appeared to be female.

The officers ordered the driver out of the vehicle, but she did not respond. Instead, she put her foot out the driver's side window and smoked a cigarette. After that, she put her feet out the door resting them on the ground outside the driver's door.

For ten minutes the officers tried to talk her into getting out of the car. At about the same time, the police were getting information on the stolen plates. The person whose car was stolen was the same person apparently driving the car with the stolen plates, Phillips.

After about ten minutes, the officers decided to shoot the woman in the legs with an SL6. (The SL6 is a shoulder-fired, semi-automatic firearm that fires polyurethane bullets with a force equivalent to a .44 magnum pistol. The department had classified the weapon as "less lethal"—in the same class as a beanbag gun.)

The officers decided to fire a warning shot, which hit the driver's door and left a baseball-sized dent. The officers then fired four times hitting the driver, Phillips, in the legs. After the fourth hit, Phillips slumped out of the car.

Phillips was hurt to the extent that she could not walk for about three weeks without a cane and received 30 stitches in her right ankle. No other residual injuries were reported.

The Seventh Circuit ruled that the force used here was excessive—as a matter of law. (The court refused to say whether one or two shots would have been reasonable.) Therefore, the only thing for a jury to resolve was how much to pay Phillips.

> *This is a bizarre case for several reasons:*
>
> 1. *The car was not stolen; the transportation department re-issued the same plates to Phillips as were issued to her previously stolen car. Bad idea.*
> 2. *Prior to the Seventh Circuit's decision in this case, a jury had already decided in favor of the officers, finding that there was no excessive force in this case. The jury probably thought the injuries were brought on by Phillips herself (i.e. if she had just gotten out of the car, none of*

this would have happened). After the jury found in favor of the officers, the Seventh Circuit held that the only question is "how much do the police owe"?

3. *The only justification for this decision is that there was virtually no threat. No threat = No use of bean bag gun or SL6 (and usually no justification even for intermediate force (see below). Officers should hesitate to use this level of force—or even intermediate force—when there is no real articulable threat.*

Intermediate force—batons, Tasers, and pepper spray

The most important factor in using intermediate force is that the officer generally has to be able to state an articulable threat that justifies that level of force.

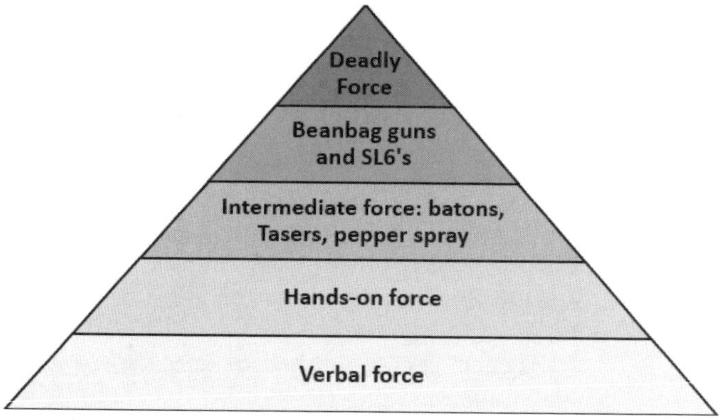

Batons

An officer's use of a baton should be reserved for situations where there is an articulable threat that an officer can state in his/her reports.

Harrington v Duszak, No. 16-4120 (7th Cir. Aug. 24, 2020)

Officers stopped the car Harrington was driving because the light over the license plate was out. Harrington then fled. Officers chased and caught Harrington. After that, one officer tased Harrington, and the other officer hit him with a baton. During that encounter, Harrington's gun fell to the ground.

Harrington sued the officers for excessive force and failure to intervene under Section 1983.

The federal district court judge ruled that the gun was admissible at the officers' trial. That probably was a big factor in the jurors ruling in favor of the officers.

The Seventh Circuit affirmed the decision of the district court.

This might be a bit extreme in the ordinary flight case.

People v Mandarino, 994 NE2d 138 (2013)

Officer Mandarino attempted to stop a car on a traffic infraction. The car stopped/parked on the driveway and passengers bailed out and went into the house. The driver was ordered to get down on the ground. The driver got on his hands and knees. The officer wanted the driver to get on his stomach. As the driver would not/did not get on his stomach, Mandarino hit him a number of times with his baton. This was all caught on Mandarino's patrol car video.

The judge found Mandarino guilty of a felony.

Streamwood and Mandarino were successfully sued under Section 1983

This is a very long opinion (66 pages or so). Approximately the first 25 pages are pictures taken from the video. Also, officers can watch the video on YouTube.

Tasers

Courts are beginning to rule that if the situation is one where officers are in a detention/traffic situation and/or the suspect is guilty only of a minor crime, officers should hesitate to use their Taser (or baton or pepper spray).

Cyrus v Town of Mukwonago, 624 F3d 856 (2010)

A lieutenant was dispatched to a partially constructed home where the owner had confronted a mentally ill person, Cyrus, who was trespassing. When the officer arrived at the home, he saw Cyrus standing outside the home. The officer asked Cyrus to come into the street and talk. Cyrus told the officer that the officer was trespassing on private property and needed to leave. The officer kept trying to talk Cyrus into discussing the matter with him in the street, but Cyrus would have none of it.

After some bantering back and forth, Cyrus turned and began to go into the house. The officer shot Cyrus in the back with his Taser. Cyrus fell to the ground. At around this time, the officer's backup arrived. Cyrus got up, and the officer tased him again. Cyrus again went down and barrel-rolled four or five times down the driveway. Cyrus ended up on his stomach. The officers ordered Cyrus to show his hands, as Cyrus' hands were underneath him. Cyrus kept his hands under him. The officers tried to force Cyrus' hands out, but to no avail. Finally the officer drive-stunned Cyrus several times (the Taser showed 12 trigger pulls total). About a minute later, they were able to handcuff Cyrus. They then rolled him over to his back and determined that he wasn't breathing.

The medical examiner found marks on Cyrus' back that were consistent with five or six taser shocks and concluded that there were eight (8) factors that contributed to Cyrus' death, several of which related to the Taser and the force used by the officers.

The officer stated that he knew Cyrus was non-violent as he had had run-ins with Cyrus on numerous occasions, none of which were violent in any way.

The Seventh Circuit Court of Appeals, applying the GRAHAM V CONNOR'S factors ruled that:

- The crime was very minor, at most a misdemeanor.
- The threat was virtually non-existent, especially when Cyrus was on the ground and there was a backup there.
- Cyrus did resist, but only to the extent of retreating into the house and having his hands under him.

Therefore, the officer could not avail himself of qualified immunity and was required to go to trial or settle the case.

People v Kotlinski, 959 NE2d 1230 (2011)

An officer stopped a car because the tags were expired. The officer smelled a lot of alcohol coming from the passenger compartment. The driver, wife, said that they were coming from a New Year's Eve party and that she was the designated driver, but that her husband, Kotlinski, was drunk. The officer got her out of the car to do some sobriety tests. Just as the officer was going to have the wife blow into the PBT, the husband got out of the car to find out what was going on. Officers ordered him back into the car many times (but never told him that they were going to arrest him if he did not get back in the car). After about 45 seconds, he got back into the car and put his seatbelt on. During this process, the officer dealing with the wife put her in handcuffs and placed her in the back seat of the patrol car, telling her that she was not under arrest. He then pulled the husband out of the vehicle, tased him several times, and arrested him for obstructing. (PS: After this, the wife blew a zero.)

A jury voted to convict Kotlinski for obstructing. But the Illinois Appellate Court reversed, ruling that obstructing requires the mental state of "knowingly" obstructing. The state never proved that Kotlinski knowingly obstructed. Therefore, the charges were thrown out.

> *The Kotlinskis sued, and Mundelein settled. You can see this whole scenario unfold on YouTube. Officers in this situation should consider whether it is a good idea to arrest if the passenger is already back in the car and seatbelted in.*
>
> *Also, try to make sure you are in an arrest situation by explaining to the suspect, if possible, that you are going to arrest him if he does not get back into the car. Then give him an opportunity to obey your lawful order, if possible. Normally, do not tase occupants of vehicles just to get them out of the vehicle—unless you can state a threat.*

Abbott v Sangamon County, 705 F3d 706 (2013)
Officers went to Abbott's home as Travis Abbott had committed an arrestable offense. Travis' mother, Cindy, arrived home and brought Travis out of the house. The officers handcuffed Travis and put him in the patrol car. Travis began to kick at the window and got the handcuffs in front of him.

At about the same time, the transportation officer accidentally hit Cindy's car with the patrol car as Cindy's car was parked right behind him. Cindy said, "I can't believe you hit my vehicle" and started to walk toward her car screaming.

The officer who hit her car got out of the patrol car and told her twice to stop, but Cindy kept walking toward her car screaming. The officer then tased Cindy in the stomach. Cindy fell down and onto her back. The officer told her to roll over. When she did not, the officer tased her again. Officers then rolled her over and handcuffed her.

The officer said he tased her because of the threat posed by the son, and the officer thought Cindy might be going to help him.

The Seventh Circuit Court of Appeals ruled that the officer may have (mistakenly) believed that Cindy was going to help her son, and, therefore, the first tase was constitutional. The second tase was unconstitutional since, using the *GRAHAM* factors, the crime was minor, there was **no threat**, and the resistance was, at worst, passive non-compliance.

Lawrence v Lewandowski, 2011 WL 940358, 2011 U.S. Dist. LEXIS 27263
An officer was told that a man who had just robbed a convenience store was running in his direction. The officer saw a man, Lawrence, running and told him to get on the ground. Lawrence slipped, fell down, and hit his head. The officer asked Lawrence where the weapon/knife was. Lawrence responded, "What knife?" Lawrence was trying to explain his innocence and was pulling his pockets out to show there was nothing in them when the officer hit Lawrence with a taser shot. The officer may have tased Lawrence more than once and then handcuffed him.

The Federal District Court (Seventh Circuit) ruled that even if the officer did tase Lawrence more than once, it was constitutional under the circumstances. The officer reasonably believed he was dealing with an armed robber who was reaching for pockets. Therefore, summary judgment was granted, and the case was dismissed.

Armstrong v Pinehurst, 810 F3d 892 (4th Cir 2015)
Officers had commitment papers for Armstrong, who was very mentally ill. When officers had originally approached him to talk, Armstrong was eating grass and dandelions and putting cigarettes on his tongue.

When the police began to take Armstrong into custody, Armstrong sat down and wrapped himself around a post that was supporting a stop sign. The officers could not pry Armstrong's arms and legs off of the post.

Within a minute or so, an officer stun-tased Armstrong. The taser had no effect, except to make Armstrong hold on tighter. The officer tased him five times during a two-minute span. Finally, five officers pulled Armstrong from the pole. The officers positioned Armstrong on the ground face down. Armstrong's sister heard her brother say that the officers were choking him. She said that the officers were pulling on his collar. An officer put his knee in Armstrong's back while cuffs were applied. The officer also stood on Armstrong's back. The officers then noticed that Armstrong was not moving. They soon figured out that the reason he wasn't moving was that he was dead.

The Federal Court of Appeals ruled that the officers violated Armstrong's rights under the Graham factors, as there was no crime and there was no threat.

Regarding the resistance, the court, citing a Ninth Circuit case, had this to say, "'Even purely passive resistance can support the use of some force, but the level of force an individual's resistance will support is dependent on the factual circumstances underlying that resistance. And here, the factual circumstances demonstrate **little risk**."

"Tasers are proportional force only when deployed in response to a situation in which a reasonable officer would **perceive some immediate danger** that could be mitigated by using a taser." Later in the case the court discusses the use of pepper spray by officers and the fact it cannot be used without some "threat" to the officers.

In conclusion, the court says that they "decline to equate conduct that a police officer characterized as resistance with an objective threat to safety entitling the officer to use a taser" (or pepper spray or a baton).

Estate of Corey Hill v Miracle, 853 F3d 306 (6th Cir 2017)
Medical personnel could not control Corey Hill, who was experiencing extremely low blood sugar levels. Hill became very combative, even ripping out the IV from his arm causing blood to spray all over from the open vein. Hill also began to kick, swing, and swear at the paramedics.

A deputy arrived and told Hill to settle down or he would be tased. When Hill refused to comply, the deputy drive-stunned tased Hill on his thigh. Hill then calmed down and was very apologetic.

However, Hill claimed his worsening diabetes condition was caused by the Taser, and he died.

The Federal District Court ruled that the officer did not deserve qualified immunity under the GRAHAM V CONNOR criteria as there was no crime or real threat, only resistance, by Hill.

The Sixth Circuit Court of Appeals ruled that there should be a new set of rules related to medical emergencies:

- Was there a medical emergency that rendered the person incapable of making a rational decision and that posed an immediate threat of serious harm?
- Was a degree of force necessary to ameliorate the immediate threat?
- Was the force used more than reasonably necessary under the circumstances?

The court ruled in this case that the officer did not violate Hill's constitutional rights and that even if he did, there was no case on point that would have put the officer on notice that he was violating Hill's rights. So the officer deserved qualified immunity.

This is non-jurisdictional as it is not a Seventh Circuit case. But it is a great idea that we can all hope the Seventh Circuit will gravitate toward.

Brooks v Seattle, 599 F3d 1018 (2011)
An officer stopped Brooks because she was driving too fast in a school zone. Brooks denied she was going too fast. She also said she was stopped because she was an African American. She refused to sign the citation, an arrestable offense in Washington. A sergeant came to the scene and tried to persuade her to sign the ticket, but she was adamant and continued to refuse. During this period, she told the sergeant that she was pregnant and had to go to the bathroom. The sergeant then told the officer to "book her." The officer attempted to get Brooks out of the car but she would not budge. Meanwhile she was pounding her horn and yelling for help.

The officers decided to apply the Taser in stun mode, first to her thigh, then to her arm, and finally to her neck. After this, they were able to handcuff her.

Brooks sued under Section 1983, alleging excessive force. The Ninth Circuit Court of Appeals, meeting en banc (all 29 judges), ruled that the officers violated Brooks' Fourth Amendment rights. Using the GRAHAM V CONNOR'S factors the court found:

- The crime was not severe/serious;
- **There was <u>no real threat</u> to the officers**;
- There was resistance—but not enough to justify tasing.

But since there were no cases at the time that would have put the officers on notice of the violation, the officers were given qualified immunity. Also, this is a 9th Circuit case – so is non-jurisdictional.

Mattos v Agarano, 661 F3d 433 (2011)
Jayzel Mattos and her husband, Troy, had a domestic dispute. Their 14-year-old daughter called the police. When the police arrived, Troy, who was 6'3" and weighed about 200 pounds, was sitting outside the door drinking a beer. The officers asked to speak to Jayzel. When Troy went in to get Jayzel, the officers followed. Troy angrily told the officers to get out of the residence. An officer then stated that Troy was under arrest.

By now Jayzel was in front of Troy. She asked that they all step outside the residence to talk. As the officer went to arrest Troy, "he [the officer] pushed up against Jayzel's chest at which point she extended her arm to stop her breasts from being smashed against the officer's body."

The officer then asked her if she was "touching an officer?" The officer at this juncture, without any warning, tased Jayzel. Jayzel fell to the floor. Troy and Jayzel were arrested, but all charges were dropped.

Jayzel sued under Section 1983 arguing the officers used excessive force. The Ninth Circuit Court of Appeals using ***GRAHAM*** ruled that the officers violated Jayzel's Fourth Amendment rights in that:

1. Her crime was not serious.
2. "Most important" **<u>Jayzel was not a threat</u>**.
3. Jayzel, at worst, "minimally resisted."

But since there were no cases at the time that would have put the officers on notice of the violation, the officers were given qualified immunity. Another 9th circuit case.

Pepper Spray/Pepper Balls

"Courts often have held that it is reasonable to use pepper spray against a suspect who is physically resisting arrest; conversely, when the use of pepper spray is gratuitous or unprovoked, courts often have considered it excessive." Brooks v Aurora, 653 NE2d 478 (2011)

Brooks v Aurora, 653 NE2d 478 (2011)

Officers (thought they) saw Brooks driving a car. Brooks' license was suspended. The officers got an arrest warrant for Brooks. Later the officers saw Brooks at a party at his home. Much of the following action was caught on police car video. As an officer told Brooks he was under arrest, Brooks began to backpedal. Facing the officer, Brooks put his arms straight out at his sides as if giving up. Then Brooks lowered his arms to his stomach level. About ten seconds after Brooks began to backpedal, the officer fired a burst of pepper spray into Brooks' face. The officer fired a second burst, and Brooks fell over a chair and landed face down on the ground, incapacitated.

The Seventh Circuit Court of Appeals ruled that even if the pepper spray constituted excessive force, "controlling law would not have communicated to a reasonable officer the illegality of applying pepper spray to an arrestee who has ceased active, physical resistance for a couple of seconds but has not submitted to the officer's authority, has not been taken into custody and still arguably could pose a threat of flight or further resistance."

> *Brooks presented apparently reliable evidence that the car was broken down during this period, so he could not have been driving it. The court assumed that the car was not drivable at the time the officers said they saw Brooks driving it. But the court held that even if that arrest was without probable cause, Brooks did not have the right to resist his arrest.*

Backes v Peoria Heights, 662 F3d 866 (7th Cir 2011)

Backes had a fight with his wife and was suicidal. He drove around, parked, and fell asleep. His wife called police. He apparently, according to his wife, had weapons. Officers tried for two hours to get a response from Backes in his car, but nothing. Police decided to shoot pepper balls into the car. Backes later filed a Section 1983 alleging that the force used was excessive.

The Seventh Circuit Court of Appeals ruled that the officers were entitled to summary judgment.

Duran v Cicero, 653 F3d 632 (7th Circuit 2011)

Officers received phone calls from neighbors about a noisy party in the Duran's back yard. The party was a celebration related to the Duran's daughter, who had just been baptized. There were about 100 guests at the party.

Police had visited the Durans at an earlier date about noise and improperly parked cars, so the relationship was tense. The conversation at the party quickly became heated between the officers and the partygoers. The officers ordered the Durans to shut down the party.

A person at the party threw a beer bottle at one of the officers. Relatively soon there were officers from four departments at the home. Most guests went into the house. The officers followed and, among other things, blasted pepper spray throughout the home.

Seventy-eight partygoers filed suit for excessive force, etc. under Section 1983.

The Seventh Circuit Court of Appeals ruled that the officers were not entitled to summary judgment. At trial, a jury awarded punitive damages to the plaintiffs (probably, in part, because someone at the party videotaped some of the conduct of the officers and because officers seized some of the cameras and then "lost" them).

Pointing a gun at someone
Pointing a gun is judged under the excessive force doctrine. In order to point a gun, the officer must have probable cause and a good, articulable reason to be concerned for his/her safety. Guns may also be drawn during reasonable suspicion stops or detentions when the detainee is violent or the crime is serious or violent.

If you draw your gun and you are concerned about the constitutionality of your act, holster your gun when you are safe and let the person know that he is not under arrest. Make sure he acknowledges that and (most importantly) be sure to put in your report that the suspect acknowledged that he knew he was not in custody.

Baird v Renburger, 576 F3d 340 (7th Cir 2009)
Officers executed a warrant at an auto body shop where the officers had probable cause that there was at least one car that had its VIN modified or removed. The officers could not point to any specific reason to believe that anyone in the auto shop would be armed.

An officer, while rounding up everyone in the shop and nearby shops, pointed his 9 mm submachine gun at the employees there. Everyone was detained about two hours.

A number of those present filed Section 1983 actions against the officer.

The Seventh Circuit Court of Appeals found the force used to be "clearly excessive" as, under GRAHAM, the crime was not violent, the detainees were all compliant and nonthreatening, and none of them tried to resist or escape. Therefore, the officer did not deserve qualified immunity.

Robinson v Solano County, 278 F3d 1007 (2002)
Robinson, a retired officer, lived in a rural area where he raised livestock and other animals. One morning he saw two dogs attacking and killing his livestock, so he shot the dogs. The owner of the dogs called the sheriff's office. The deputies who were dispatched were told that Robinson just shot two dogs with a shotgun and that Robinson was in the middle of the road yelling. Soon thereafter six patrol vehicles pulled up to Robinson's home. Robinson, wearing an unbuttoned shirt and a pair of jeans, walked out to meet the officers.

The officers testified that Robinson appeared agitated, so the officers unholstered their guns. Robinson testified that he was calm and that the officers originally came up to talk to him without drawing their guns.

When Robinson told the officers that he was the man who killed the dogs, the officers pointed their guns at him. The officers told Robinson to put his hands on his head and pointed their guns at his head at a distance of four feet. Robinson asked why they were doing that. When Robinson put his hands on his head, the officers handcuffed him and put him into the back seat of a patrol car. The officers never searched Robinson, they never frisked Robinson when they first saw him, and they did not search him after the arrest.

Robinson tried to explain the situation, but the officers refused to listen to him. Later, the officers realized that Robinson had broken no law, and they released him.

Robinson filed an excessive force claim.

The district court granted summary judgment for the officers. The court held that the officers were entitled to qualified immunity from Robinson's excessive force claims because they "have no dependable guidance upon the constitutional limitations, if any, upon a mere threat or display of force to effect a seizure."

The Ninth Circuit ruled that a prior case law gave officers notice that "putting a gun to a suspect's head at point blank range can constitute excessive force" [that case was McKenzie v Lamb, 738 F2d 1005, 1008 (9th Cir. 1984)]. The Ninth Circuit held that there was a genuine issue of material fact, so there could be no summary judgment or qualified immunity. Therefore, the Ninth Circuit reversed and remanded the case in order to have a jury decide whether the officers' conduct was reasonable.

McDonald v Haskins, 966 F2d 292 (1992)
An officer, while lawfully searching a house, pointed his gun at the head of a nine-year-old boy and threatened to pull the trigger.

The Seventh Circuit Court of Appeals ruled that the officer could not avail himself of qualified immunity. Therefore, the case would have to be decided at trial or settled.

Mentally Ill Suspects
Officers are experiencing more and more mentally ill persons. These people are unpredictable. Most are non-violent. The problem for officers as it relates to Section 1983 actions is that officers must generally have a standard approaching probable cause to believe the mentally ill person is a danger to himself or others to take him into custody. The officer must also be sure to try not to hurt the person, as mentally ill people present a very sympathetic plaintiff for a jury. If there is time, always try to get someone out who can talk to a mentally ill person if you do not know how.

If you are ever sued for excessive force dealing with a mentally ill person, make sure your attorney is aware of the *Turner* case:

Turner v. City of Champaign, No. 19-3446 (7th Cir. Nov. 3, 2020)
Turner was a homeless man and was well known to the police. On prior occasions, the police had him hospitalized without any struggles. The police were called to check on Turner, who was walking in the street, talking to people, and rummaging through garbage cans.

An officer saw Turner on a street corner rolling around with his pants down. Turner began flailing his arms and babbling unintelligibly. As other officers arrived, Turner began jaywalking and started walking across the street several times. The officers decided to detain Turner and to send him to a hospital for mental health treatment, so they called for an ambulance. Before the ambulance arrived, an officer asked Turner to sit on the curb.

Turner ran away. Officers chased Turner, and they ended up in an alley. Because Turner did not stop, an officer grabbed his shoulder. Turner pulled away and shoved an officer. A struggle ensued, and eventually Turner was taken to the ground and handcuffed. Turner began kicking his legs, so an officer placed leg restraints on him. Officers then noticed Turner was not breathing. The ambulance arrived, and Turner was taken to the hospital. On the way to the hospital, Turner died. The autopsy showed no signs of suffocation or trauma. Turner died as a result of cardiac arrhythmia—his heart gave out after beating too fast during the encounter. Turner had an enlarged heart and an insufficient blood supply to one of his heart's chambers that likely caused the cardiac arrhythmia.

Turner's estate sued the officers under Section 1983 for Fourth Amendment violations.

The district court judge found that the officers did not use excessive force and granted summary judgment in favor of the police officers.

The Seventh Circuit agreed that the officers did not use excessive force.

The court gave only lip service to GRAHAM V CONNOR. This is very important as, if the officers would have been righteously judged under GRAHAM, the officers probably would have lost as there was no crime and no real threat.

First, the court addressed the question of whether the police had a right to detain Turner. The court stated, "a mental health seizure is lawful if there is probable cause to believe that the person is a danger to himself or others." The fact that Turner was disoriented, was speaking unintelligibly, and was repeatedly crossing the street carelessly gave the officers probable cause to seize him.

Second, since the officers had a legal right to seize Turner, they could also use reasonable force to accomplish the seizure. The court addressed whether the police had a right to bring Turner to the ground and restrain him. The court found that Turner was actively resisting the officers and that at each step of the encounter with Turner the officers used reasonable force.

Estate of Biegert v Molitor, 968 F.3d 693 (2020)
Biegert's mother called police explaining that Biegert texted her, stating that he was suicidal and had taken a number of pills. Biegert was depressed and had a history of suicide attempts. His mother said he was alone and had no weapons.

When the officers got to Biegert's apartment, Biegert would not let them in at first. After entry, the officers wanted to be sure that Biegert had no weapons on his person, so they began to pat him down. Biegert resisted. At that point a free-for-all ensued where one officer tased the other officer. Biegert grabbed a knife and cut one officer's arm. The other officer pulled his sidearm and stepped back. Biegert stepped toward the officer with the knife. The officer shot and killed Biegert. It was only two minutes from entry to the shooting.

The federal district court judge ruled that the officer(s) deserved summary judgment.

The Seventh Circuit, while criticizing the officers for their failure to have a plan before confronting Biegert, decided that the officers deserved summary judgment.

King v Hendricks County, 954 F.3d 981 (2020)
Bradley King was 29 years old and suffered from paranoid schizophrenia. He called 911 requesting help. Two deputies responded to perform a "welfare check" and help in any way they could.

As they approached Bradley's home, Bradley came out, walked toward one of the officers, and pulled a 10-inch kitchen knife (from King's kitchen) out of his pocket, which he held in his left hand. The officers backed up, drew their guns, and told him to drop the knife. As Bradley ran toward one of the officers, the officer shot and killed Bradley. The knife was later observed to be near Bradley's left hand. There were no fingerprints on the knife.

Bradley's father Matthew, said that Bradley was right-handed and would not have held a knife in his left hand. Also, Matthew said that Bradley had never been violent and would not have charged the deputies.

Matthew brought a Section 1983 action against the deputy, the County Commissioners, the Sheriff's Department, and the Sheriff. There were no witnesses to the shooting, so there was no material dispute of facts.

The district court judge granted summary judgment for the officer and all other defendants.

The Seventh Circuit ruled that Matthew's alleged facts were no more than "speculation or conjecture." So the court affirmed the district court's holding that the officer deserved summary judgment.

Pena v Leombruni, 200 F3d 1031 (1999)
A man shoplifted and acted "crazy" in a store. An officer arrived and could see the man, Pena, was mentally unstable. When Pena confronted the officer in a threatening manner, the officer felt compelled to pepper spray the man and his dog. Pena then picked up a chunk of concrete. The officer back-pedaled and told the man to put the concrete down. When Pena was within five to ten feet, the officer shot Pena and killed him.

Pena's administrator sued the officer for excessive force, arguing that the officer should have been trained to handle mentally ill or unstable people without shooting them.

The Seventh Circuit Court of Appeals ruled that the officer may respond with deadly force if the officer reasonably believes that he is in imminent danger of great bodily injury or death. Therefore, summary judgment was appropriate.

Cyrus v Town of Mukwonago, 624 F3d 856 (2010)
An officer was dispatched to a partially-constructed home where the owner had confronted a mentally ill person, Cyrus, who was trespassing. When the officer arrived at the home, he saw Cyrus standing outside the home. The officer asked Cyrus to come into the street and talk. Cyrus told the officer that the officer was trespassing on private property and needed to leave. The officer kept trying to talk Cyrus into discussing the matter with him in the street, but Cyrus would have none of it.

Cyrus then turned and began to go into the house. The officer shot Cyrus in the back with his Taser. Cyrus fell to the ground. At around this time, the officer's backup arrived. Cyrus got up, and the officer tased him again. Cyrus again went down and barrel-rolled four or five times down the driveway. Cyrus ended up on his stomach. The officers ordered Cyrus to show his hands, as Cyrus' hands were underneath him. Cyrus kept his hands under him. The officers tried to force Cyrus' hands out, but to no avail. Finally the officer drive-stunned Cyrus several times (the Taser showed 12 trigger pulls total). About a minute later, they were able to handcuff Cyrus. They then rolled him over to his back and determined that he wasn't breathing.

The medical examiner found marks on Cyrus' back that were consistent with five or six taser shocks and concluded that there were eight (8) factors that contributed to Cyrus' death, several of which related to the Taser and the force used by the officers.

The officer stated that he knew Cyrus was nonviolent as he had had run-ins with Cyrus on numerous occasions, none of which were violent in any way.

The Seventh Circuit Court of Appeals, applying the GRAHAM V CONNOR'S factors, ruled that:

- The crime was very minor, at most a misdemeanor.
- The threat was virtually non-existent, especially when Cyrus was on the ground and there was a backup there.
- Cyrus did resist, but only to the extent of retreating into the house and having his hands under him.

Therefore, the officer could not avail himself of qualified immunity and was required to go to trial.

Estate of Williams v The Indiana State Police Department, 797 F3d 468 (7th Cir 2015)
Family members called police to their home because Williams had threatened to commit suicide and had locked himself in the bathroom. Williams had already cut himself and said that it was taking too long to bleed out. He had taken a number of Xanax pills, and he threatened to kill anyone who came into the bathroom. The officers unlocked the door and tried to subdue Williams with a taser. The taser didn't work. Williams then attacked the officers with a knife. The officers shot and killed Williams.

The Seventh Circuit Court of Appeals ruled that the officers in this case deserved qualified immunity as there was no case at the time that would have put the officers on notice that their conduct was unconstitutional.

Brown v Blanchard, 31 F Supp 3d 1003 (7th Cir 2016) (A companion case to the Williams case above.) Basically the facts are similar to the *Williams* case, above, in that Brown had told people he was thinking of committing suicide, had locked himself in the bedroom, and had a knife nearby. Brown was bipolar and had not taken his medication. He also had drunk a lot of alcohol.

The *Brown* case is different from *Williams* in that in the *Brown* case:

- Nancy Brown, his mother, had previously entered the room and hugged Brown and talked to him.
- The officers did not first attempt to use less than deadly force.
- The officers could see Brown through a window and could see that Brown was not hurting himself—but that he had a knife and alcohol nearby.
- The officers broke in the door and shot Brown.
- Nancy Brown did not hear the officers give any commands to Brown before shooting him.

The Seventh Circuit Court of Appeals ruled that the officers here did not deserve qualified immunity as there was a "material" question of facts (which only a jury can resolve) in that Brown's mother said the officers did not tell Brown to drop the knife. Also, Brown's mother testified that Brown was not aggressive and that she had previously held her son's head. So the court basically held that a jury might rule that Brown did not charge the officers with a knife.

Santos v Gates, 287 P2d 846 (2002)
Officers were told that a man, Santos, was "screaming and falling down in the street." A woman also said that Santos might have taken something from a neighbor's garage down the street.

When officers arrived they saw that Santos was screaming and walking erratically. The officer accosted Santos. Santos was instructed to turn around and put his hands on his head. Santos was "passive." Santos turned around but dropped his hands to his sides. An officer then grabbed Santos' wrists to handcuff him. Santos apparently went limp to the ground and began to yell: "They're beating me, they're beating me like Rodney King."

It was soon determined that no burglary had occurred.

Three paramedics took Santos to the hospital where it was determined that his back/vertebra had been broken. Doctors later testified that the vertebra had been broken near the time when the police subdued Santos, but could not testify with certainty that it was the police who caused the injury.

Santos sued the officers and the department for violation of his Fourth Amendment rights under Section 1983.

Relying on GRAHAM, the Ninth Circuit found:

- The crime suspected was not serious. At most, Santos was guilty of public intoxication. (The officers had no idea where the garage was or what had allegedly been stolen.)
- Santos did not pose a safety risk or a threat; the officers described him as "passive."
- There was no indication of active resistance from Santos.

The Ninth Circuit ruled that qualified immunity was not available to the officers and stated: "[W]e have held on many occasions that summary judgment or judgment as a matter of law in excessive force cases should be granted sparingly."

> *When Santos began to complain of excessive force, the officers called their supervisor. The supervisor obtained statements from several eyewitnesses. The supervisor never filed a report about the incident. The defendants did not introduce the supervisor's interviews at all, leaving the impression that the interviews went badly for the officers.*

Drummond v Anaheim, 343 F3d 1052 (2003)
Officers went to Drummond's home in response to Drummond's fiancé's plea that Drummond was paranoid and hallucinating. Drummond had run out of medications for his mental illnesses. The officers determined that Drummond was not a danger to himself or others and refused to take him to the hospital.

The next night Drummond was worse. Drummond's neighbor called the police fearing that Drummond was going to run into the street in front of traffic.

The officers who responded called for an ambulance and then knocked Drummond to the ground and cuffed him. Drummond offered no resistance. One officer put his knees and weight on Drummond's back, and the other officer put his knees on Drummond's neck. Drummond, who weighed 160 pounds, pleaded with the officers to get off of him as he could not breathe. The officers continued to put weight on Drummond's back and neck. The officers apparently placed their weight on Drummond for some time. As a result, Drummond lost consciousness and fell into a coma from which he never recovered. He became, in effect, a vegetable.

The Ninth Circuit Court of Appeals determined that the officers were faced with a mentally ill man—not a criminal. There was no danger of serious resistance, and escape was most unlikely. The court found that there was no reason to continue to place all their weight on the man when he was cuffed and couldn't breathe. Therefore, neither summary judgment nor qualified immunity was available as defenses for the officers.

> *A reason that this conduct could cost the officers their house and car here is that witnesses testified that while Drummond pleaded for his life, the officers laughed and joked about Drummond's condition.*

Maag v Wessler, 960 F2d 773 (1991)
Maag worked with toxic pesticides and was acting strangely. He lacked coordination, had slurred speech, and acted irrationally. He wandered off, and when he returned he insisted on driving. The police were called, and then the police called a doctor. The doctor said to bring Maag to the hospital. Maag resisted and had to be restrained in handcuffs. When a doctor examined Maag, the doctor said Maag was uncooperative and was incapable of carrying out logical thinking. Maag defecated on himself while at the hospital.

Maag filed a Section 1983 action under the Fourth Amendment. The Ninth Circuit Court of Appeals ruled that the officers "had probable cause to take Maag into protective custody... Therefore, they (were) immune."

Officers should check with their departmental rules and attorneys regarding the issue of handling the mentally ill.

Traffic Stops

The occupant of a vehicle does not have the "right" to refuse to get in or out of the vehicle when ordered to do so by an officer. Officers should be very careful about exercising their discretion in this circumstance—or the courts will take away the power over occupants in vehicles.

Officers must use reasonable force in such circumstances, however. It is strongly advised that if an occupant of a vehicle refuses to get out of the vehicle during a traffic stop, the officer should call for a backup, give warnings ("I will be forced to arrest you if you don't get out of the car now."), and arrest the occupant first before pulling him/her out. Officers should not use their Tasers or pepper spray in this situation unless there is some articulable threat to their safety.

Davis v Clifford, 825 F3d 1131 (2016)

Officers stopped a woman, Davis, who had an arrest warrant for driving on a suspended license for failure to provide proof of insurance. After Davis stopped in a parking lot, the officers surrounded her with their cars. The officers apparently hit her car with batons. Davis, who had a handicapped symbol, rolled up her windows and locked her doors. Officer Clifford told her to step out of the car. She asked why she had been stopped, and the officer responded that she knew why and told her she was under arrest. Clifford then ordered her to "step the fuck out of the car." She said she would if the officers promised not to hurt her. An officer then smashed her window with his baton and pulled her out of the car through the window by her hair and arms. Officers laid her on the ground face down on the glass and handcuffed her.

The federal appellate court ruled that the officers were not entitled to summary judgment / qualified immunity implying that the force used was excessive under the circumstances.

The court relied on the GRAHAM factors [GRAHAM V CONNOR, 490 US 386 (1989)], ruling that:

- the crime deserved "minimal force,"
- Davis did not appear to be a threat at all, and
- Davis did not present an escape risk as she was surrounded by police cars. She did resist by rolling up her windows, but she stated she was afraid and simply said she would get out and asked that she not be hurt.

One of the main cases cited as precedent by this court was Cyrus v Mukwonago, 624 F3d 856 (2010), the seminal Seventh Circuit case discussing excessive (non-deadly) force.

Brown v Bryan Co, 219 F3d 450 (2000)

An officer saw a truck make a 180-degree turn in order to avoid a roadblock. The officer chased the truck for a short distance. The driver of the truck stopped. The officer ordered the female passenger out of the truck. When she leaned forward, the officer used an "arm bar" to get her out. The officer then spun her to the ground. She landed on her knees on the street and was severely injured. The officer testified that Brown did not struggle or resist in any way. Brown testified that she was trying to comply with the officer's demands before he pulled her out.

At trial, the jury was informed that the officer had only been on the force for a short period, had little training, and had himself been arrested prior to his being hired as an officer. The Fifth Circuit Court of

Appeals ruled that neither summary judgment nor qualified immunity were appropriate. A jury ruled in favor of Brown and against both the officer (for excessive force) and against the city (for failure to train). The jury awarded Brown about a quarter million dollars.

> *Any time you need to use force to get an occupant into or out of the vehicle, you should be prepared to explain why it was necessary to use the amount of force you used. You may use "reasonable" force to remove an occupant—not unreasonable force. And you should use force only after you have warned the occupant that he/she will be arrested for obstructing.*

People v Synnott, 811 NE2d 236 (2004)
Officer Driscoll stopped Synnott's car because it was speeding. The officer obtained Synnott's license and proof of insurance. He then asked Synnott to shut off the engine. Synnott did not comply. The officer asked Synnott "if he would prefer to sit on the curb." Synnott asked if he was under arrest. The officer then asked if he would prefer that. Synnott said he would not. The officer again asked Synnott to shut off the engine. Synnott shut off the engine. The officer thanked Synnott and walked back to his police car.

Officer Driscoll called for a backup and went back to talk to Synnott. Driscoll asked Synnott to step out of the car. Synnott asked again if he was under arrest. Driscoll responded that he was not. Synnott then said that his lawyer told him never to get out of the car. The officer then instructed Synnott that he had no right to stay in the car during a traffic stop and that he must get out. The officer also warned Synnott that if he didn't get out of the car, he would be arrested.

After four warnings, Synnott grabbed the steering wheel with both hands. Driscoll then grabbed Synnott's left arm and pulled him out of the car.

The Illinois Appellate Court ruled that a person does not have the right during a traffic stop to remain in the car when he is ordered to get out. Therefore, Officer Driscoll did not violate Synnott's rights, and his conviction for obstructing was affirmed.

> *Be sure to warn the driver that he will be arrested for obstructing. Do not abuse your power here.*

People v Kotlinski, 959 NE2d 1230 (2011)
An officer stopped a car because the tags were expired. The officer smelled a lot of alcohol coming from the passenger compartment. The driver, wife, said that they were coming from a New Year's Eve party and that she was the designated driver but that her husband, Kotlinski, was drunk.

The officer got her out of the car to do some sobriety tests. Just as the officer was going to have the wife blow into the PBT, the husband got out of the car to find out what was going on. Officers ordered him back into the car many times. <u>The officers never said they were going to arrest him if he did not get back in the car.</u> After about 45 seconds, he got back into the car and put his seatbelt on. During this process, the officer dealing with the wife put her in handcuffs and placed her in the back seat of the patrol car, telling her that she was not under arrest. He then pulled the husband out of the vehicle, tased him several times, and arrested him for obstructing. (PS: After this, the wife blew a zero.)

A jury voted to convict Kotlinski for obstructing. But the Illinois Appellate Court reversed, ruling that obstructing requires the mental state of "<u>knowingly</u>" obstructing. The state never proved that Kotlinski knowingly obstructed. Therefore, the charges were thrown out.

> ***General rule**: <u>Do not tase unless you can state some kind of threat</u>. A Section 1983 suit was brought against the Mundelein officers involved. Mundelein settled.*

Brooks v Seattle, 599 F3d 1018 (2011)
An officer stopped Brooks because she was driving too fast in a school zone. Brooks denied she was going too fast. She also said she was stopped because she was an African American. She refused to sign the citation, an arrestable offense in Washington. A sergeant came to the scene and tried to persuade her to sign the ticket, but she was adamant and continued to refuse. During this period, she told the sergeant that she was pregnant and had to go to the bathroom. The sergeant then told the officer to "book her." The officer attempted to get Brooks out of the car, but she would not budge. Meanwhile, she was pounding her horn and yelling for help.

The officers decided to apply the Taser in stun mode, first to her thigh, then to her arm, and finally to her neck. After this, they were able to handcuff her.

Brooks sued under Section 1983, alleging excessive force.

The Ninth Circuit Court of Appeals, meeting "en banc" (all 29 judges), ruled that the officers violated Brooks Fourth Amendment rights. Using the GRAHAM V CONNOR'S factors, the court found:

- The crime was not severe/serious;
- **There was no real threat to the officers**;
- There was resistance—but not enough to justify tasing.

But since there were no cases at the time that would have put the officers on notice of the violation, the officers were given qualified immunity.

Handcuffs
Generally, if an arrestee gets hurt during a handcuffing, the officer may be successfully sued, unless the arrestee resists during the handcuffing.

Handcuffing without probable cause or exceptional circumstances is usually unconstitutional and subject to constitutional law suits. Once again, it is important to know that the Seventh Circuit has issued a warning about handcuffing when you don't have probable cause to arrest.

> *"Although we have upheld the use of handcuffs to ensure officer safety in a Terry stop of brief duration, without automatically escalating the situation to an arrest, that does not mean that law enforcement has a carte blanche to handcuff routinely. The proliferation of cases in this court in which Terry stops involve handcuffs and ever-increasing wait times in police vehicles is disturbing, and we would caution law enforcement officers that the acceptability of handcuffs in some cases does not signal that the restraint is not a significant consideration in determining the nature of the stop." Ramos v Chicago, 716 F3d 1013 (7th Cir 2013)*

But if there is reasonable suspicion to believe that the suspect is violent or committed a violent offense, it is constitutional to handcuff briefly (even though there is no probable cause).

Howell v Smith, 853 F3d 892 (2017)
Officer Smith received a dispatch about an alleged road rage incident where the driver of a tan Trailblazer had fired at the victim. The victim explained that the suspect was a white male with facial hair and was alone in the vehicle.

Officer Smith saw the vehicle and driver that matched the description and conducted a "high-risk" stop—i.e., the driver, Howell, was required to walk backwards, kneel, and be handcuffed. Howell apparently told the officers that his shoulder was sore.

The victim was brought to the scene and confirmed that Howell was the person who fired at him.

The officers searched Howell and Howell's vehicle but could not find a gun. The officers then decided to release Howell. Howell had been held in handcuffs for about 30 minutes.

Howell sued under Section 1983, alleging that he had suffered mental anguish and several shoulder-related surgeries since the stop. However, during a deposition, Howell said that he never told the officers he was in "pain." He simply said his shoulder was sore.

Officer Smith sought summary judgment, arguing that he should receive at least qualified immunity.

The federal court judge ruled that there was a question of fact related to the amount of force that was administered (and only juries can resolve issues of fact), and, therefore, Officer Smith could not be permitted relief based on qualified immunity.

The Seventh Circuit ruled that during this stop on reasonable suspicion, the officer had good reason to handcuff Howell (as the crime was violent), and Howell failed to explain to the court how the handcuffing was excessive (so no factual dispute really on whether the force was excessive). Therefore, the district court's decision was reversed and summary judgment awarded Officer Smith.

Another issue is using Tasers to control arrestees who have been handcuffed.

Wate v Kubler, 839 F3d 1012 (2016)
Barnes, who stood 5'10" and weighed 290 pounds, was in the water when he became erratic and started to yell loudly about a demon. Many people around him and on the beach became concerned. An officer nearby saw a man try to reason with Barnes and get him to leave the water. Barnes would not. The officer believed that he had probable cause to arrest Barnes for battery on one of the men there.

The officer entered the water and ordered Barnes out of the water. When Barnes would not get out, the officer hit Barnes in the face many times. Barnes continued to resist.

The officer finally brought Barnes to shallow water and placed a handcuff on one wrist. Barnes then attempted to drag the officer to deeper water. The officer continued to hit and drag Barnes out of the water.

The officer then tried to secure Barnes' other wrist with the handcuff, but Barnes continued to resist. Finally with the help of bystanders, the officer handcuffed Barnes. By this time Barnes was struggling to breathe and blood and fluids spewed from Barnes' mouth.

Barnes continued to resist and bit the officer, so the officer continued to hit Barnes. During this period, the officer called for back-up. When back-ups arrived, Barnes was starting to "wear down" according to one witness and wasn't fighting as much.

Barnes was placed on his stomach, but he kept raising up, so an officer put his knee on Barnes' back. Another back-up officer told Barnes that he would employ his Taser if Barnes didn't stop resisting. The officer deployed the Taser five times over a two-minute period. After this period, Barnes became inert. There was a dispute among the witnesses as to when Barnes went inert.

An off-duty fire lieutenant saw that Barnes was bluish gray and told the officers to uncuff Barnes and begin CPR. Barnes died two days later.

The District and Federal Courts of Appeals ruled that the officer who tased Barnes should not be afforded the protection of qualified immunity as Barnes was secured and the officer's deployment of the Taser five times appeared to be excessive.

> *The other issue here is whether handcuffs were too tight or if the handcuffing procedure was intended to hurt the arrestee unreasonably [Hansen v Black, 885 F2d 642 (1989)].*

Arpin v Santa Clara Valley, 261 F3d 912 (1998)
A woman, Arpin, was arrested and handcuffed. She brought a 1983 action alleging that the handcuffs and the handcuffing procedure hurt her. She stated that the officer twisted her arm behind her "with enough force to lift her off the ground and break her watch band." The officers/defendants responded that Arpin "stiffened her arm when being handcuffed, which caused the officers to use additional force." The trial/district court held that summary judgment should be granted to the officers/defendants.

The Ninth Circuit Court of Appeals ruled that Arpin could not "provide specific facts to show that the force used was unreasonable or that she sustained actual injuries." Therefore, the district court opinion was affirmed.

Hansen v Black, 885 F2d 642 (1989)
Officers responded to a robbery. The footprints in the snow from the robbery led the officers to Hansen's residence. Two officers watched the house while other officers went to get a warrant.

According to the police, Kathleen Hansen came out of her home in the early morning with garbage and began to put it in the garbage truck. The officers started to take the garbage from the truck, and Hansen tried to stop them. Officer Black told Hansen that, if she didn't stop hindering him, she would be arrested. Hansen then looked at the officer and said "son of a bitch." Hansen was then arrested.

Hansen, on the other hand, filed an affidavit that said she did not physically or verbally hinder the officers from removing the garbage from the truck. She stated also that she was at least 75 feet from the officers. She also said that she said "son of a bitch" to her mounds of garbage, which had not been removed from her driveway.

A neighbor filed an affidavit that stated that the officers were in a different driveway from Hansen when all the talk went on. And that there was the garbage man between Hansen and the officers.

The district court granted summary judgment for the officers.

The Ninth Circuit Court of Appeals reversed ruling that there was a genuine issue of material fact related to the cause for the arrest, which could only be resolved by a jury.

Finally, the neighbor filed an affidavit that the officers used undue force in handcuffing her: "He was rough and abusive." Hansen was later treated for injuries resulting from the handcuffing. There were obvious bruises on her wrists and arms.

The Ninth Circuit ruled that summary judgment was inappropriate. The excessive force case must go to the jury for resolution.

Noisy Parties
Noisy parties are becoming an expensive problem for officers across the country. Illinois has case law that holds that noisy parties, even noisy underage parties, are not exigencies which would permit entry. (See People v Eden and People v Olson in the premises chapter.)

The Seventh Circuit Court of Appeals has not been sympathetic to requests for qualified immunity for officers who enter drinking parties and hurt guests. Some of these have gotten very expensive for the departments, even resulting in punitive damages. See e.g. Duran v Cicero, 653 F3d 632 (7th Circuit 2011).

Use of dogs to seize/arrest persons

The rule related to the use of dogs is probably: the more dangerous the criminal and his crime, the more likely the use of a dog to subdue him will be constitutional (see Chew v Gates, below).

The less serious the crime, the more likely the use of a dog will be viewed as excessive [e.g. Marley v City of Allentown, 774 F Supp 343 (ED Pa 1991), where the court ruled that the use of a police dog to pursue a suspected misdemeanant was unreasonable].

Mendoza v Block, 27 F3d 1357 (1994)

Mendoza robbed a bank and escaped in a car. He then abandoned the car and fled on foot. He ran about a half mile and hid under some bushes on private property for several hours. The officers told Mendoza that he should come out or they were going to send a dog/Rottweiler in after him. The dog caused some injury to Mendoza.

Mendoza brought a Section 1983 action claiming excessive force was used, in that the officers encouraged the dog to bite even after Mendoza surrendered, etc. The officers, of course, denied these allegations.

The Ninth Circuit ruled that the officers were protected by qualified immunity as Mendoza was dangerous to both the officers and nearby property owners. Furthermore, Mendoza fought with the dog thereby increasing his pain.

The court noted that, had there been evidence to show that the dog was permitted to bite Mendoza after he had surrendered, Mendoza would have had a cause of action, and the officers would not have been allowed to claim qualified immunity.

Chew v Gates, 27 F3d 1432 (1994)

Officers stopped Chew on a traffic offense, but Chew ran off into a scrap yard. The officers determined that Chew had three felony warrants (but the officers never stated what the warrants were for—serious or non-dangerous offenses). Officers warned Chew to surrender or the officers would send their "chew" dog after him. The dog was a German Shepard trained to seize suspects by biting and pulling. It was also trained to attack and bite and pull if a person was concealed. Chew was obviously hiding and so got chewed up.

Chew also alleged that he surrendered and that Officer Bunch ordered the dog to attack Chew. The officers said that Chew refused to surrender and hit the dog with a pipe. The officer admitted that he kicked Chew.

The district court granted summary judgment to the defendants except Bunch. The jury rendered a verdict and damages against Bunch.

The Ninth Circuit Court of Appeals ruled that, in addition to Bunch's liability, the city could be liable if the city teaches and has an unconstitutional policy related to dogs biting and seizing all suspects.

The Ninth Circuit ruled, however, based on Mendoza above that police chief, trainers, and supervisor of the training unit were entitled to qualified immunity.

Use of flash-bang grenades

The use of flash-bang grenades should be avoided unless the suspect is dangerous.

Escobedo v Bender, 600 F3d 770 (7th Cir 2010)

Escobedo was suicidal. He had a gun and said he didn't want to hurt anyone, and that he desperately wanted to talk to someone about his drug addiction and life circumstances. A negotiator talked to Escobedo. The deputy chief decided to use tear gas, because negotiations appeared to be going nowhere, pedestrian and vehicle traffic was increasing, and Escobedo was apparently beginning to barricade himself in. The deputy chief apparently testified that he wasn't aware that Escobedo had said that he didn't want to hurt anybody, including police.

The police then swarmed Escobedo's residence while setting off tear gas and flash bang grenades. Escobedo then shot and killed himself.

Escobedo's estate brought suit under Section 1983.

The Seventh Circuit ruled that although there was no Seventh Circuit case directly on point, officers knew, or should have known, that when a suspect does not present a threat to officers, the use of this much force cannot be justified under qualified immunity. Therefore, the motion for qualified immunity was denied.

Interfering with an arrest

Officers may use reasonable force to stop anyone interfering with a lawful arrest.

Dawson v Brown, 803 F3d 829 (7th Cir 2015)

Officers were arresting Dawson's son after he fled from officers during the officers' attempt to execute a traffic stop. During the struggle on Dawson's driveway, Dawson (the father) approached the officers and "showed his hands" indicating that he did not have a weapon. An officer deployed his taser on the son, but it didn't work. He was about to deploy it again when the father came within three or four feet of the fight and said, "Please don't kill him." He also put his hand on an officer and told him, "Leave my son alone; don't hurt him." The officer told Dawson to get back, and kicked Dawson in the side. Dawson stumbled backward and was then tackled by another officer.

Dawson was arrested for resisting and obstruction. But he was never formally charged. He went to the emergency room for injuries he sustained.

Dawson filed six counts against the officer(s) under Section 1983, mostly related to excessive force.

The Seventh Circuit Court of Appeals ruled that there were no material facts at issue. Therefore, the case could be settled as a matter of law. It was reasonable for the officer to "believe that Dawson was attempting to interfere with a lawful arrest." Therefore, the officers were granted summary judgment as they had not violated Dawson's rights as a matter of law.

Sexual contact, etc.

Once a female is in custody and she is being transported, it is difficult to disprove charges of sexual abuse. Therefore, whenever sexual improprieties are alleged, it is almost impossible for an officer/defendant to be granted a summary judgment.

Fontana v Haskin, 262 F3d 871 (2001)

Fontana was arrested. She alleged that during her transportation to the jail she was sexually harassed and touched by Haskin.

The Ninth Circuit Court of Appeals ruled that her claim, if proved, is a violation of her Fourth Amendment rights. Therefore, the case must go to trial.

The admissibility of a DUI conviction

A DUI conviction is admissible in a trial where officers are sued for excessive force during the detention and arrest. Sanchez v City of Chicago, ___F3d___ (7th Cir 2018)

Seizures of property

In the vast majority of cases where officers seize evidence unconstitutionally, the issue is a search question. Sometimes, however, the issue is held to be a seizure question.

SOLDAL V COOK COUNTY, 113 S Ct 538 (1992)
The owner of a mobile home park filed an eviction proceeding against Soldal. Before the owner got a judgment from the court, the owner got the Sheriff's deputies to help in seizing the mobile home.

The United States Supreme Court ruled that the seizure of Soldal's home was unconstitutional. Therefore, Soldal had a cause of action against the officers and their department under Section 1983.

Bell and Spinks v Chicago, 835 F3d 736 (2016)
Bell was driving Spinks' car when officers arrested Bell, apparently on drug charges. There was probable cause to believe the car contained drugs. Officers seized the car for forfeiture.

The Seventh Circuit ruled that a vehicle may be seized under Chicago's forfeiture ordinance if there is probable cause that the vehicle has drugs in it or has been used in a drug transaction.

Pepper v Village of Oak Park, 430 F3d 805 (2005)
Pepper and her husband became estranged, and the husband was thrown out of the house. The husband needed to retrieve some items of property from the home and called the police for an "escort." An officer arrived and stood by while the husband took many items of property from the wife that did not belong to him, but were on a forged rental agreement reflecting that the husband needed to get the property back to the rental company. The wife was not home.

The wife sued under Section 1983 alleging that the officer lacked training in this area and that the officer helped her husband to seize her property.

The Seventh Circuit Court of Appeals ruled that the officer did not seize anything. The seizure was conducted by a "private" person. Therefore, the officer and the department were awarded summary judgment.

> *The result could be different if the wife had been home and objected to the seizure of the property. Try to get people who want to retrieve their property to get an order on the exact pieces of property from the court. Also, get the person entering the home to agree in writing that if the person in the home disagrees as to ownership, it must be decided in court. If there are any disagreements that aren't clear, make the people argue it out in court.*

Siebert v Severino, 256 F3d 648 (2001)
An officer received a call that horses at the Siebert farm were not provided with shelter or water. The officer went into the Sieberts' barn, which was 60 feet from the house and was surrounded by a fence. The officer checked on the welfare of the horses and left a notice at the Sieberts' premises, because the Sieberts had failed to provide adequate shelter and protection for the horses. Three days later, many officers returned and loaded up several horses in a trailer.

The district court granted summary judgment for the defendant/officer, but the Ninth Circuit Court of Appeals reversed, ruling that the officer(s) violated the Fourth Amendment rights of the plaintiffs (the Sieberts) by entering the barn without a warrant. The court further held that the law in this area was so well settled that the defendant, Severino, could not claim qualified immunity.

The Ninth Circuit also ruled that the seizure of the horses was unconstitutional, as the officers could not prove any exigency/emergency for the seizure. Again, the court held that qualified immunity was not available to the officer as the law in the area was well settled.

Miranda v Cornelius, 429 F3d 858 (2005)
Mr. Miranda was attempting to teach Mrs. Miranda how to drive by permitting her to drive their car around the block. Mr. Miranda had a valid driver's license. Mrs. Miranda had no driver's license. An officer saw the car being driven poorly and at 10 mph. So the officer stopped the car just as it was being driven onto the Miranda driveway.

The officer cited Mr. and Mrs. Miranda and then impounded and towed the car, pursuant to a city ordinance that permitted the towing of a car when the driver has no valid license.

The Mirandas sued the officer, his department, etc., under Section 1983 for towing/impounding the car.

The Ninth Circuit ruled that qualified immunity for the officer was not available in this circumstance.

Jackson v Chicago, 975 NE2d 153 (2013)
A woman apparently loaned her car out to two men who were later found by police to be parked and smoking marijuana. An officer arrested the men and discovered cannabis in the passenger compartment. The car was then forfeited under ordinance.

Jackson argued that seizure of her car violated her Fourth Amendment rights.

The Illinois Appellate Court disagreed stating that even if she had no idea that the car was being used to commit an illegal act, the seizure did not violate her Fourth Amendment rights (or her due process rights). Therefore, the seizure was constitutional.

Moral? Be careful who you loan your car to.

Harrington v Heavey, (___ F Supp___ 2009 non pub)
An officer stopped Harrington for speeding. Harrington's driver's license was expired because he failed to renew it. Harrington's mother showed up at the scene and asked that the car be released to her. She had a valid license, insurance, and registration. The officer towed the car under a local ordinance.

Mrs. Harrington sued under Section 1983.

The Federal District Court in Illinois ruled that the impoundment was unconstitutional and that qualified immunity was not appropriate in that any officer should know that "impoundment (in this circumstance) is permissible only when the arrestee was not able to provide for immediate removal of the vehicle." Therefore, summary judgment was denied.

Fuller v Vines, 36 F3d 65 (1994)
Officers were lawfully investigating an incident when they passed by Fuller's front yard. The officers said that Fuller's dog, Champ, charged at the officers, so the officers shot and killed the dog. Fuller alleged that the dog did not move at all toward the officers.

Fuller then said, when he objected to the shooting, that an officer pointed the gun at Fuller's head and threatened to kill him by stating that he (the officer) was going to send Fuller "to the morgue." Fuller backed off and the officers left.

Fuller sued under Section 1983.

The Ninth Circuit Court of Appeals ruled that there was no seizure in the constitutional sense in that Fuller was free to leave. According to everyone, there was no arrest or TERRY stop. The officer was simply taking no chances that Fuller would attack him (the officer). Therefore, summary judgment was properly granted on that issue.

The Ninth Circuit further ruled that there was a material question of fact on the issue of the seizure of the dog (did the dog attack the officers or not?). Therefore, that issue was remanded for a jury trial.

Brown v Muhlenberg, 269 F3d 205 (2001)
An officer shot Brown's Rottweiler. Witnesses said that the Rottweiler was not acting aggressively in any way. Brown sued the officer.

The Third Circuit Court of Appeals ruled that neither summary judgment nor qualified immunity were available to the officer, as there was a material difference between the officer's testimony and that of the witnesses. Therefore, the case had to go to a jury or be settled.

V. Searches

Unreasonable searches can result in Section 1983 actions against officers. Often these searches involve the search of homes or intrusive body searches, like strip searches. However, any unreasonable search can be the subject of a Section 1983 action.

MONROE V PAPE, 365 US 167 (1961)
Officers entered Monroe's home unconstitutionally. The officers then required the residents to stand naked while officers searched every room. Mr. Monroe was taken to the station and unconstitutionally questioned about a murder.

The United States Supreme Court ruled that Monroe had a cause of action under Section 1983 for the unconstitutional search (and seizure).

Officers who understand the "search" concepts in the early chapters of this text, and follow the rules outlined in the text, will not likely violate a suspect's rights such that they will be sued.

If a search is arguably not violating the Fourth Amendment at the time of the search, the officers or other state agents conducting the search will be immune from suit.

Montville v Lewis, 87 F3d 900 (1996)
City building inspectors saw evidence of city code violations from outside Montville's home. They knocked on the door, and the contractor working on the premises answered the door. The inspectors asked to enter the home. The contractor agreed, and the inspectors entered and found evidence of other violations. Montville sued the inspectors for violation of her Fourth Amendment rights.

The court ruled that the inspectors were entitled to qualified immunity under the Fourth Amendment proposition that the inspectors reasonably believed that the contractor had the authority to consent to the search (even though he did not). Therefore, the suit was thrown out.

Officers would probably be held to a higher standard, as any officer would (or should) know to inquire further about the authority of such persons to consent. (A close case though.)

Searches of persons

Officers must have a doctrine or theory to be able to search a person constitutionally.

Strip and body cavity searches

These are areas where officers should exercise extreme caution—rules differ depending upon the department and jurisdiction.

It is crucial in this area that officers know the associated statutes, ordinances, and their departmental rules—and follow them.

The Constitution does not prohibit strip searches of arrestees who are going to be integrated with the jail population.

FLORENCE V BOARD OF CHOSEN FREEHOLDERS, 132 S Ct 1510 (2012)
An officer executed a bench warrant by arrest for Florence for failure to pay a fine, a minor offense. He was later strip searched and deloused before entering the jail population. Florence sued.

The United States Supreme Court ruled that this procedure was constitutional if the arrestee is going to be integrated into the jail population.

"Strip searches of persons arrested for minor offenses are [normally] prohibited by the Fourth Amendment, unless reasonable suspicion exists that the arrestee is carrying or concealing contraband or suffering from a communicable disease" [Karim-Panahi v Los Angeles Police Department, 839 F2d 621 (1988)].

Do not assist welfare workers if they intend to undress children, unless the social worker has obtained a warrant or there are exigent circumstances.

Kimberly v Gresbach, 526 F3d 1008 (2008)
Social workers heard that the principal of a private school gave spankings. They went to the school and demanded to see certain students. The case workers interviewed the students and required them to disrobe.

The Seventh Circuit Court of Appeals ruled that this was unconstitutional and refused to grant qualified immunity (citing Karim-Panahi v Los Angeles Police Department).

Searches of premises

Officers who enter premises (an area where a suspect has a reasonable expectation of privacy) without a valid warrant, exigency, or consent may be successfully sued under Section 1983.

Search versus no search—reasonable expectation of privacy

If an officer intrudes into an area where a suspect/citizen has a reasonable expectation of privacy, the officer has conducted a "search" under the Fourth Amendment. (To conduct a search, an officer must have a warrant, be faced with exigent circumstances, or obtain voluntary consent.

CARROLL V CARMAN, 135 S Ct 348 (2014)
Officers obtained information that a wanted criminal was residing at the Carman's home. The house was on a corner, so the front of the house faced one street, and the side of the house faced the other street. The house had a front and side (sliding glass door) facing the street(s).

Officers, including Officer Carroll, went to the sliding glass door (instead of the front door) and knocked. The Carmans came out of the house, and an altercation ensued.

The Carmans sued under Section 1983 for entering an area (without a warrant, exigency, or consent) where the Carmans could reasonably expect privacy.

The Federal Court of Appeals ruled that any officer should know that the sliding glass door on the side of the house should not be the first option for a knock and talk. Therefore, Officer Carroll could not avail himself of qualified immunity.

The United States Supreme Court reversed, ruling that Officer Carroll was entitled to qualified immunity (as there was no case on point that would have put the officer on notice that he was doing anything unconstitutional.)

LOS ANGELES V MENDEZ, 137 S Ct 1539 (2017)
Officers, searching for an armed and dangerous parolee, look into a known inhabited shanty in a back yard and come face to face with two people and a gun pointed at them.

The district court and the Ninth Circuit Court of Appeals believed that officers should have known that they cannot enter outbuildings of a home without a warrant, exigency / emergency, or consent. These courts felt the officers should be liable under the "provocation" doctrine, which provides that it was the illegal, unconstitutional act of the officers that "provoked" the incident.

The United States Supreme Court specifically ruled that the entry of the shanty was unconstitutional and officers can be sued for that conduct as they had no warrant or consent and they failed to announce.

Frane v Kijowski, 992 F Supp 985 (ND IL 1998)
A 17-year-old girl called police stating that her father, Frane, was beating up her mother. She stated further that her father might be playing with her BB gun. The dispatcher failed to relay the information to the officers about the BB gun. An officer peeked through the kitchen window and saw that Frane was holding a gun to his wife's head. The officer then shot Frane. After entering, the officers determined that the gun was a BB gun.

Frane sued the officer, one cause of action being the officer's search of the house by peeking in the window.

The Seventh Circuit Court of Appeals ruled that the officer's peeking into the window was a search. However, it was a reasonable search under the emergency doctrine.

Cook v O'Neill, 803 F3d 296 (2015)
Officers were investigating a nasty, "ugly" (the court's words) home invasion-robbery. They had arrested one perpetrator. When they searched his phone, they discovered several calls to Thede.

The officers went to Thede's home nine days after the crime. They rang the doorbell at the building entrance, and Thede buzzed them in. She met them in the hallway in her pajamas. The officers asked her if anyone else was in her apartment. She replied, "a friend." She asked to re-enter her apartment to put on some clothes. The officers said she could. She then re-entered the apartment and either closed the door or left it slightly ajar. The officers opened the door or opened it further in order to see into the apartment. The officers heard her talking to someone in the apartment. They yelled for her to bring the person to the living room so they could see him.

When Cook appeared, the officers immediately recognized him as the perpetrator. So the officers entered the apartment and arrested him.

Cook sued under Section 1983 for Fourth Amendment violations, especially entering premises without a warrant. The entry would have been unconstitutional except that Cook had an arrest warrant out for him, so the court decided to give the officers qualified immunity. Also, Cook may not have had a reasonable expectation of privacy in Thede's home.

Siebert v Severino, 256 F3d 648 (2001)
An officer received a call that horses at the Siebert farm were not provided with shelter or water. The officer went into the Sieberts' barn which was 60 feet from the house and was surrounded by a fence. The officer checked on the welfare of the horses and left a notice at the premises because the Sieberts had failed to provide adequate shelter and protection for the horses. Three days later, many officers returned and loaded up several horses in a trailer.

The district court granted summary judgment for the defendant/officer, but the Ninth Circuit Court of Appeals reversed, ruling that the officer violated the Fourth Amendment rights of the plaintiffs by entering the barn without a warrant or emergency. (The court further held that the law in this area was so well settled that the defendant, Severino, could not claim qualified immunity.)

Conner v City of Santa Ana, 897 F2d 1487 (1990)
Officers without a warrant or any search theory went onto Conner's premises in order to copy the VINs of vehicles being stored there. In order to view the VINs, the officers had to scale the fence.

The Ninth Circuit ruled that the officers could be successfully sued for that unconstitutional search. The jury awarded $71,000 in compensatory damages.

Search theories or doctrines
An officer must have a valid warrant, be faced with an exigency/emergency or have valid consent to enter areas around premises where a suspect/citizen has a reasonable expectation of privacy.

The (arrest or search) warrant requirement

Sparing v Olympia Fields, 266 F3d 684 (2001)
An officer had probable cause to arrest Sparing. The officer went to Sparing's home and knocked on the door. Sparing came to the door and stood inside it. The officer told Sparing that he was under arrest. Sparing asked if the officer had a warrant. The officer responded that he did not; that he had probable cause. Sparing turned around and walked away from the screen door and back into his home. The officer then entered Sparing's home and arrested him.

Sparing sued the officer under Section 1983 for violation of his Fourth Amendment rights.

The Seventh Circuit Court of Appeals ruled that the officer violated Sparing's constitutional right to be free from the unreasonable search of his home.

Hadley v Williams, 368 F3d 747 (2004)
Hadley sexually assaulted minors. Detective Williams wanted to arrest him. Williams called Hadley's home and talked to Hadley's mother. Williams asked Hadley's mother if the police could enter the home to arrest Hadley. Hadley's mother responded that she would permit the entry, only if the officers had a warrant. Williams said, "Yes, we've got everything we need. It's all covered." So Hadley's mother agreed. In fact, the officers did not have an arrest warrant or any other kind of warrant.

The officers entered the home and arrested Hadley. Hadley was convicted and sentenced to 20 years in prison.

Hadley sued because he was arrested in violation of the Fourth Amendment when the officers entered his home without a warrant.

The federal district court ruled that the detective deserved summary judgment.

The Seventh Circuit Court of Appeals reversed, ruling that summary judgment could not be awarded, as it was clear that the detective violated Hadley's rights and that any reasonable officer would know that it was a violation.

Exigency/emergency

SAN FRANCISCO V SHEEHAN, 135 S Ct 1765 (2015)
Sheehan lived in a room in a facility for people with mental illnesses. A social worker stopped in to see Sheehan in her room, as Sheehan had stopped taking her medication and was no longer changing her clothes or eating. Sheehan told the social worker that she had a knife and would kill him if he didn't leave.

The social worker left and called the police. The social worker then sought—and received—help to get Sheehan to a hospital for treatment as she was obviously a danger to other people.

An officer arrived but realized quickly that she needed backup and called her sergeant. The two of them entered Sheehan's room after knocking and announcing their purpose. They told her when they knocked that they wanted to help her. Sheehan grabbed a 5-inch kitchen knife and told the officers that she was going to kill them. The officers retreated out of the room, and Sheehan closed the door.

The officers heard sirens, indicating more backup was on the way. The officers decided to immediately re-enter and subdue Sheehan before backup arrived. The officers entered Sheehan's room with pistols drawn. The sergeant immediately pepper sprayed Sheehan. When Sheehan attacked the officers with a knife, the officers shot her.

The prosecutor could not get a conviction against Sheehan, and Sheehan sued under Section 1983 for entering her room without a warrant and excessive force.

The Federal District Court ruled that the officers should be accorded summary judgment on the exigency issue because they had to act quickly in that they didn't know if:

- Sheehan would go out the back window (although she was on the second floor) or
- Whether there was someone else in Sheehan's room whom Sheehan might harm or
- Whether she might hurt herself.

The Ninth Circuit Court of Appeals reversed ruling that there was "no objective need for immediate entry." The Ninth Circuit decided that the officers "provoked" the response from Sheehan, and, therefore, the case must go to a jury.

The United States Supreme Court basically agreed with the District Court on the facts supporting the emergency entry; but ruling that, even if the officers were wrong, they deserved qualified immunity, concluding that everyone has 20/20 hindsight and that it's easy to second guess officers in this very tense circumstance.

RYBURN V HUFF, 132 S Ct 987 (2012)
There was a rumor floating around the high school that Vincent Huff was going to bring a gun and "shoot up" the school. Someone said there was a note, but no one seemed to know where the note was. Kids at school took the threat seriously and were staying home.

Officers decided to go to Huff's home to investigate. Officers called Mrs. Huff, who was very reluctant to speak with the officers. They asked her to come out front of the house, and she hung up on them.

Soon thereafter, Vincent and Mrs. Huff came outside the front door and talked to the officers. Vincent totally denied the threat accusations. When the officers asked Mrs. Huff if there were guns in the home, she turned and ran into the house. The officers followed her. Mr. Huff then told the officers to get out of the house. The officers said they would not—until they were satisfied that there was no threat to the children at the school.

After 10 or 15 minutes the officers apparently determined that the rumor was untrue and left the home.

The Huffs sued under Section 1983.

The United States Supreme Court ruled that the officers deserved qualified immunity as there was no case at the time that would have put the officers on notice that they could not enter the Huff residence in this circumstance.

> *This case is sort of worthless to officers as the court never says whether the officers' conduct was constitutional or not. In our opinion, it was not.*

Hawkins v Mitchell, 756 F3d 983 (7th Cir 2014)
Officers were dispatched to a "domestic." When the officers arrived at the residence, the officers saw a woman who had been locked out of her boyfriend's house. She said that her boyfriend, Hawkins, had her keys, including her car keys. She said that Hawkins had not physically assaulted her in any way. She was just afraid that Hawkins would get violent. So she called 911.

The officers knew that Hawkins had a history of abusiveness and drunkenness. The officers knocked on Hawkins' door to try to retrieve the woman's keys. Hawkins said he didn't have her keys and that the officers must leave. Hawkins began to shut the door, and an officer stuck his foot in the door. The officers then entered Hawkins' premises. Hawkins told the officers to leave many times while talking to his attorney on the phone. An officer told Hawkins that if he didn't get off the phone, he would be arrested. Hawkins continued talking on the phone to his attorney. The officers arrested Hawkins.

Prosecutors dismissed the case, and Hawkins sued under Section 1983.

The Seventh Circuit Court of Appeals ruled that there was no theory for entering Hawkins home, and, therefore, the officers could not receive summary judgment.

White v Stanley, 745 F3d 237 (7th Cir 2014)
A sheriff's deputy, Tammie Stanley, pulled Nancy Hille over for an expired vehicle registration sticker early in the morning hours. When Stanley ran the plates, she determined that the plate's expiration date was different than the date on the expired sticker. She could not reconcile the date discrepancy because of the lateness of the hour. So she released Hille.

The next day, Deputy Stanley determined from the Secretary of State that the sticker on Hille's car was stolen. That is a class 4 felony. Stanley and a fellow officer, Morrison, went to Hille's home to arrest her. Hille lived with her boyfriend, White.

When the officers knocked on the door, White, the owner, answered. The officers explained to White that they wanted to come in and speak to Hille. White adamantly refused to let them in without a warrant.

The officers then said they smelled marijuana burning inside, so they entered based on that (exigency). ("Indeed, Hille had been smoking marijuana just before the officers arrived." In fact, she still had the joint in her hand when the officers entered and arrested her.)
White tried to shut the door on the officers, but they pushed through after Officer Stanley put her foot in the door. White then retreated up the stairs. Morrison caught White. White claimed injuries resulted. The officers then arrested both White and Hille.

The Federal District Court ruled that there was no exigency and that the officers were not entitled to qualified immunity.

The Seventh Circuit Court of Appeals agreed that "the smell of burning marijuana, without more, did not create an exigency permitting these officers to make a warrantless entry." The Court, however, decided that the officers deserved qualified immunity because there was not enough case law on point to put the officers on notice that such entries were unconstitutional.

Finally, the court issued a warning to officers who want to enter premises based on the smell of marijuana in the future:

> **"Future police officers faced with a situation like the one confronting Stanley and Morrison should not feel emboldened to act as the deputies did here. Henceforth, officers who make a warrantless entry under the circumstances found in this case should expect no shelter from liability."**

The excessive force claim by White is apparently pending in Federal District Court.

Hamrick v Lewis, 539 F Supp 1156 (DC IL 1982)
Officers had probable cause to believe Hamrich was in possession of—and probably selling—drugs. They also suspected that Hamrich had a weapon. The officers had information that Hamrich was going to leave town the next day.

Officers tried to get in touch with a state's attorney, but with no luck. The officers entered Hamrich's home at 4:30 a.m. As Hamrich was flushing the drugs, an officer shot and killed him.

The Federal District Court ruled that the officers were not entitled to qualified immunity.

Calabretta v Floyd, 189 F3d 808 (1999)
A neighbor of Calabretta told a social worker that Calabretta must be hitting his children, because the neighbor heard a child say "No, no, no!" and "No, Daddy, no!" late at night.

Four days later the social worker went to Calabretta's home to check on the children's welfare, but Mrs. Calabretta wouldn't let the social worker in.

Ten days later the social worker got a police officer to accompany her to Calabretta's home. Mrs. Calabretta didn't want to let them in since Mr. Calabretta was not home. The social worker and the officer entered without consent. The officer went with the mother and the social worker talked to the 12-year-old and the 3-year-old. Both kids said that their mother would sometimes hit them with a round wooden dowel. The social worker then instructed the 12-year-old to strip the 3-year-old in order to see if there were marks on the buttocks. The 12-year-old refused. The mother was then required to pull down the 3-year-old child's pants.

The Ninth Circuit Court of Appeals ruled that neither the social worker nor the officer could avail themselves of qualified immunity. Both should have known that in order to enter a home they must have a warrant, exigency/emergency, or consent.

Never permit anyone to tell you that the rules of search and seizure do not apply to you. They do.

Alexander v City and County of San Francisco, 29 F3d 1355 (1994)
Public health officials obtained an inspection (administrative type) warrant to investigate a sewage leak at a house. When they attempted to serve the warrant, a man inside said that he was going to "get my gun and use it." The SWAT team was called in and they broke into the house. The man tried to shoot the SWAT team (but his gun misfired). The SWAT team then shot and killed the man.

The Ninth Circuit Court of Appeals ruled that the officers did not appear to have a warrant (arrest or search) or consent to enter the premises before the shooting. The case was reversed and remanded to determine whether there were exigent circumstances and whether unreasonable force was used to enter the house.

The court ruled that the officers could escort the health officials in the investigation of the sewer, but that it appeared to be "massive disproportionality" if the only issue was a leaky pipe.

Penilla v City of Huntington Park, 115 F3d 707 (1997)
Penilla became seriously ill while sitting on his porch. Officers arrived and found Penilla to be in serious need of medical services. The officers then broke into Penilla's home and (sort of) deposited Penilla there. The next day Penilla's family members found Penilla dead.

Penilla's estate sued under Section 1983 for Fourth and Fourteenth Amendment violations. The defendant officers moved to dismiss based on qualified immunity. The district court ruled that there was no legal basis for entering the house because the only reason for entering was to deposit Penilla there. The officers could not resort to the exigency/emergency doctrine to support the entry/search.

The Ninth Circuit affirmed. (Therefore, qualified immunity was not appropriate, and the case was remanded for a jury trial on the illegal search.)

Thompson v Mahre, 110 F3d 716 (1997)
Officers knocked and announced but did not wait before serving a warrant, because they knew that the resident was very violent and had a gun. During the execution of the warrant, officers shot the resident's dog and a fellow officer.

The district court suppressed the evidence and refused to grant summary judgment for the officers in the 1983 case. The district court then instructed the jury that the officers violated the plaintiff's rights by failing to knock and announce.

The Ninth Circuit Court of Appeals ruled that the decision as whether the officers should be granted qualified immunity should be resolved by the jury even if the court has denied the officer summary judgment based on that. Furthermore, the Ninth Circuit ruled that, as a matter of law, the officers were entitled to qualified immunity, so the court reversed the decision of the district court [see SAUCIER V KATZ, 121 S Ct 2151 (2001), for the law now].

Baker v Clover, 864 P2d 1069 (1993)
The trial court ruled that the officer had followed a DUI suspect into his garage unconstitutionally. Therefore, Baker was awarded damages and attorney's fees.

The Arizona Court of Appeals ruled that an officer might not have been aware that a garage was protected by the Fourth Amendment, because at that time in Arizona there was no case law or statute directly and specifically on point. Therefore, the officer was protected by qualified immunity, and the trial court's judgment was reversed.

Frane v Kijowski, 992 F Supp 985 (ND IL 1998)
A seventeen-year-old girl called police stating that her father, Frane, was beating up her mother. She stated further that her father might be playing with her BB gun. The dispatcher failed to relay the information to the officers about the BB gun. An officer peeked through the kitchen window and saw that Frane was holding a gun to his wife's head. The officer then shot Frane. After entering, the officers determined that the gun was a BB gun.

Frane sued the officer, one cause of action being the officer's search of the house by peeking in the window.

The Seventh Circuit Court of Appeals ruled that the officer peeking into the window was a search. However, it was a reasonable search under the emergency doctrine.

Leaf v Shelnutt, 400 F3d 1070 (2005)
A person called 911 and hung up. An officer went to the person's home. The caller said that he heard glass breaking at a nearby apartment. When he confronted Leaf (the person breaking in), Leaf said rudely that he was breaking into his own apartment.

Officers went to the suspect's apartment. When no one responded, the officers entered and searched the apartment. When they nudged Leaf, the resident, who was sleeping, Leaf jumped up with a 15-inch bowie knife and attacked the officers. The officers shot and killed Leaf.

The district/trial court ruled that the officers could not get qualified immunity on the entry.

The Seventh Circuit Court of Appeals ruled that qualified immunity was appropriate, as the officers reasonably did not realize that they their entry was unconstitutional. Therefore, the case was dismissed.

Hanson v Dane County, 608 F3d 335 (7th Cir 2010)
Someone called 911 and hung up. The dispatcher called back, but no one answered. Officers went to the home, but the female who called could not remember why she called. The officers entered to make sure everyone was okay and questioned the residents even though the residents asked the officers to leave.

The Seventh Circuit Court of Appeals ruled that it was reasonable for officers to enter under these circumstances and ask questions of everyone until it could be established whether or not a crime had been committed. Although Hanson was in custody, the answers he gave were never used in court. Therefore, the officers were given summary judgment by the court.

Finsel v Cruppenink, 326 F3d 903 (2003)
Finsel checked into a hotel and then parked his truck next to his room. When the motel manager came on duty, she determined that the truck was blocking access. The manager asked and then told Finsel to remove his truck, but according to the manager, Finsel wanted his money back. Finsel hung up and refused to answer the phone. The manager sent two security people to Finsel's room, but Finsel would not answer the door.

Finally, the manager called the Sheriff's office and told a deputy what had happened. She said that she needed to get the truck moved. A deputy arrived and knocked on Finsel's door with his hand and then with his flashlight. He also identified himself as a deputy. Still, there was no response from Finsel. The deputy tried the key, but the inside chain lock was engaged. Finally, the deputy, with the manager's approval, kicked the door in. The officer then arrested Finsel.

The charges were later dropped, and Finsel sued the deputy for an unlawful search and excessive force. Finsel obtained summary judgment on the unlawful search, but not on the excessive force cause of action (for which they had to go to trial). The deputy's motion for summary judgment based on qualified immunity was denied.

The Seventh Circuit Court of Appeals found that the officer, as a matter of law, violated Finsel's Fourth Amendment right to be free from unreasonable searches by breaking into his room, as Finsel was breaking no law whatsoever. Therefore, summary judgment and qualified immunity were not available to the officer who broke into Finsel's room.

The court held that the excessive force action, etc., would have to be decided by a jury.

The hotel manager apparently changed her story a bit when it came time for testifying. Remember, witnesses usually won't help you in court. Get their statement tied in right away—preferably in writing.

The court stated that the community caretaking doctrine may apply in some circumstances when hotel employees call officers out to help, but rarely.

Finally, the court suggested that, since the only thing that was really a problem was the truck. Well, maybe that truck should have been towed.

Scope of the search
Once officers have entered premises under the authority of a legitimate legal theory, the officers must stay within their theory or find a new theory for extending the search. Usually the scope of the search is controlled by the plain view doctrine which states that, in order for an officer to seize crime-related evidence, the officer must be lawfully present in the area where the evidence is, and the officer must have probable cause to believe the evidence is crime-related.

Ruggiero v Krzeminski, 928 F2d 558 (1991)
Officers searched premises ostensibly under the consent theory, but the jury found that the search was improper because it was not conducted with the valid consent of either resident. The jury awarded damages and attorney's fees.

The officers appealed, arguing that the search fell within the theory of the plain view doctrine.

The Ninth Circuit Court of Appeals ruled that the plain view doctrine can never validate an otherwise warrantless search. To be permitted to use the scope argument or plain view doctrine, an officer must be validly in the premises. So the officers' argument was rejected.

Searches of vehicles
Officers must have a legal theory to enter vehicles—probable cause, search incident to arrest or detention, consent, or inventory.

Luellen v City of East Chicago, 350 F3d 604 (2003)
A confidential informant, who had given reliable information during the previous three years, called an officer with the East Chicago Police Department and told him that Luellen, a fireman, was gathering

absentee ballots from numerous people at a house party. Apparently the CI told the officer that Luellen had placed the absentee ballots in his car. The officer searched Luellen's trunk and found the absentee ballots.

Luellen got into lots of trouble and was fired from his job. Luellen sued for failure to have probable cause for the search.

The Seventh Circuit Court of Appeals ruled that the officers had probable cause to believe that crime-related evidence was in the vehicle. Therefore, summary judgment in favor of the officers was granted.

Miranda v Cornelius, 429 F3d 858 (2005)
Mr. Miranda was attempting to teach Mrs. Miranda how to drive by permitting her to drive their car around the block. Mr. Miranda had a valid driver's license. Mrs. Miranda had no driver's license.

An officer saw the car being driven poorly and at 10 mph. So the officer stopped the car just as it was being driven onto the Miranda driveway. The officer cited Mr. and Mrs. Miranda and then impounded and towed the car pursuant to a city ordinance that permitted the towing of a car when the driver has no valid license.

The Mirandas sued the officer, his department, etc., under Section 1983 for towing the car.

The Ninth Circuit ruled that qualified immunity for the officer was not available in this circumstance.

This is more of a seizure issue than a search issue.

Search warrants

There are a number of ways that officers are vulnerable to 1983 actions when they draft or execute search warrants.

Drafting the warrant and affidavit

Officers who write up warrants for the wrong house are normally going to be liable under Section 1983 [Navarro v Barthel, 952 F2d 331 (1991)].

Officers normally get themselves into constitutional problems where they are most vulnerable to civil suit when they misstate the facts in their affidavits.

In Hervey v Estes, the Ninth Circuit created "a standard for summary judgment on a defense request for a grant of qualified immunity in a civil rights action charging judicial deception in violation of FRANKS." Officers must pass on both of these to be granted summary judgment on the issue of qualified immunity:

- Was the warrant affidavit so deficient, as a consequence of the omissions, that no reasonable officer either would have believed that probable cause existed or would have applied for the warrant?
- Did the officer make intentional false statements or make the omissions recklessly or with the intent to deceive the issuing court with respect to probable cause?

Hervey v Estes, 65 F3d 784 (1995)
An officer in filling out an affidavit avowed that another officer was "certified" in narcotics training or clandestine laboratory investigation and also that an officer smelled "acetone" or "P2P" when he didn't.

The district court granted summary judgment for the defendants.

The Ninth Circuit Court of Appeals reversed, ruling first that the affiant either deliberately lied or was reckless, and second that without the lies there would be no probable cause. Therefore, summary judgment was inappropriate. And the affiant was not entitled to qualified immunity because, according to the court, "his conduct was thoroughly unprofessional."

Lombardi v El Cajon, 117 F3d 1117 (1997)
An officer got a search warrant for Lombardi's residence. The officer executed the warrant and discovered crime-related evidence. The judge who issued the warrant presided over the FRANKS suppression issue in the criminal case. The judge ruled that the officer had omitted some material facts. Therefore, the judge suppressed the evidence.

Lombardi then sued under Section 1983. The district court ruled that, even if the omitted information had been included, there still would be probable cause, but that there was a material factual dispute over whether the officer intentionally omitted the information. The district court therefore refused to grant summary judgment on that issue.

Proofread your warrant and affidavit. Don't exaggerate or fudge the facts. Don't omit facts that are material to the probable cause determination. Those can come back to haunt and embarrass you.

Betker v Gomez, 692 F3d 854 (2012)
An, officer, Gomez, stated in his affidavit for the search warrant a number of "facts" that the informant later avowed in testimony were untrue.

Even worse, during the execution of the warrant, officers shot the resident.

The Seventh Circuit Court of Appeals ruled that the officer could not avail himself of qualified immunity because the informant had specifically sworn under oath during deposition that she did not say the things that Gomez swore in the affidavit that she did say.

Because there was a "factual" dispute here, the dispute must be settled by a jury.

Particularity requirement
Officers must state with particularity what is to be searched and what is to be seized. Officers must proofread the warrant to be sure it is accurate. And if during the execution, officers determine that where they need to search is different than what is in the warrant, the officer must obtain another warrant. Officers must be very careful to avoid over-breadth. Do not specify items in the warrant for which you do not have probable cause. Nor should officers seek to search areas where there is no probable cause.

GROH V RAMIEREZ, 124 S Ct 1284 (2004)
Officer Groh, drafting a warrant, "failed to identify any of the items that Groh intended to seize. In the portion of the form that called for a description of the person or property to be seized, Groh typed a description of Ramierez' two-story, blue house rather than the alleged stockpile of firearms."

The United States Supreme Court ruled that summary judgment was not justified for Groh. The warrant was "plainly invalid" on its face. Therefore, the search of the home was "warrantless within the meaning of case law." That is, the Supreme Court viewed this search as no more or less than the officers barging into someone's home without any warrant at all.

The officer had accurately described the "things to be seized" in his application for the warrant, and therefore sought "qualified immunity" from liability. The Supreme Court rejected this argument, since a simple proofreading of the warrant would have solved this problem.

MESSERSCHIMDT V MILLENDER, 132 S Ct 1235 (2012)
Officers obtained a search warrant for evidence after a girl who had been domestically assaulted by a gang member told the police about the gang member's affiliation. The officers wrote up a warrant that was overbroad and executed it against the Millender home. The Millender's sued.

The United States Supreme Court ruled that, although the warrant was overbroad, the officers should receive qualified immunity, as both the prosecutor and the issuing judge saw no problem with the warrant.

Jones v Wilhelm, 425 F3d 455 (2005)
The search warrant ordered the search of the apartment on the "right" at the top of the stairs. The officer in charge of executing the warrant thought that the warrant meant the "left" at the top of the stairs. There were a number of reasons for this mistake, one of them being that there were two staircases facing in opposite directions leading up to the apartments. So the officers entered the wrong apartment (the Jones' apartment). When they learned that they were in the wrong apartment, they apologized, quickly left, and searched the right apartment.

The Seventh Circuit Court of Appeals ruled that the officers should have cleared up the facial ambiguity in the warrant before serving it, and, therefore, they were not entitled to qualified immunity on the warrant claim.

Jacobs v Chicago, 215 F3d 758 (2000)
Officers had a search warrant for a certain address. After arriving at the address, the officers determined that the building was a multi-address dwelling/apartment building. The address on the warrant only specified the whole building. The officers searched Jacobs' apartment. Jacobs sued.

The Seventh Circuit Court of Appeals ruled that the officers were not protected by qualified immunity, because the law was well-settled that officers may not enter multi-unit dwellings when they have a warrant for a building. Therefore, the case was remanded for trial.

Since the search was arguably unconstitutional, the officers also arguably detained Jacobs unconstitutionally.

Executing the warrant
Officers are vulnerable to Section 1983 suits when they fail to knock, announce and wait and when they detain non-residents too long and behave too intrusively in the premises.

It goes without saying that "officers conducting a search should read the warrant or otherwise become fully familiar with its contents" [United States v Whitten, 706 F2d 1000 (1983)]. The courts generally deny offending officers immunity if they do not determine specific information regarding what the warrant authorized them to do [Marks v Clarke, 102 F3d 1012 (1997)].

Of course, officers must use reasonable force in the seizure of persons in the premises. Handcuffing might be perfectly reasonable (see MUELER V MENNA), whereas using a submachine gun against a resident who altered a VIN would not be. Baird v Renburger, 576 F3d 340 (7th Cir, 2009).

It is especially easy for detainees to sue for excessive force as "[u]nreasonable force claims are generally questions for the jury" [Hervey v Estes, 65 F3d 784 (1995)].

If there is any doubt about whether an officer is searching the right premises, officers should stop and make sure. If the warrant does not accurately describe the premises, officers should withdraw immediately. (Guzman v City of Chicago)

Thompson v Mahre, 110 F3d 716 (1997)
Officers decided to knock and announce, but not wait when they were serving a warrant at Deshetres' residence. Deshetres had a long record of arrest for drugs, assault, robbery, interference with officers, etc. Also, a truck was just leaving the Deshetres residence as the officers arrived. The officers thought the people in the truck might notify Deshetres. The officers entered and engaged in a gun battle where people were hurt. Deshetres came out with a gun and was shot.

The district court ruled that the officers violated the plaintiff's rights and left to the jury the amount of damages. The jury decided that the sergeant who led the assault should be required to pay Deshetres $82,500 (for shooting him) and $10,000 to another resident who was frightened by the assault.

The Ninth Circuit Court of Appeals ruled that the officers reasonably believed that Deshetres would meet the officers with a weapon and would flush his drugs down the toilet. Therefore, the failure to wait was ostensibly reasonable. And the sergeant was entitled to qualified immunity as a matter of law.

Jones v Wilhelm, 425 F3d 455 (2005)
Officers knocked, announced, and waited before they entered Jones' residence with a warrant. Five officers testified at the suppression hearing. One officer testified that the officers waited two seconds between knocking and entering; another officers testified that they waited 18 seconds between the knocking and entering. The other three officers estimated times between two and 18 seconds. Mr. Jones testified that when he heard the knock, he got up to go to the door when the officers entered his apartment forcibly.

The Seventh Circuit Court of Appeals ruled that the officers' failure to wait deprived them of the defense of qualified immunity.

Ramierez v Butte Silver Bow County, 283 F3d 985 (2001)
An officer received two reports that the Ramierez household had a rocket launcher and other illegal weapons. The officer wrote up an affidavit and warrant but failed to properly fill in the blank that asked for/required the items to be searched for and seized. The officer then obtained a warrant and executed it. Nothing illegal was discovered.

Ramierez sued the officer, but the district court ruled that the officer enjoyed the protection of qualified immunity.

The Ninth Circuit ruled that the officer should have proofread the warrant. The court reversed and remanded the case for a determination by a jury as to whether a reasonable officer would have noticed the defects in the warrant.

Larez v City of Los Angeles, 946 F2d 630 (1991)
Officers (apparently unnecessarily) hurt some people and broke lots of personal property during the execution of a search warrant. One of the "victims" of the police search complained, by grievance, to the LA Police Department. The Department apparently whitewashed the investigation, and Chief Gates signed a letter reflecting that none of the allegation could be sustained.

Larez, et al, then sued the officers, the department, the chief, and the city. The plaintiffs called an expert witness to testify that the conduct of the officers was unreasonable and that the department and the chief had virtually never upheld a grievance against an LA officer.

The district court jury awarded compensatory damages to the plaintiffs against the officers and punitives ($170,000) against Chief Gates in his individual capacity.

The Ninth Circuit Court of Appeals ruled that the officers were justifiably sued and that the compensatory damages awarded by the jury were justified.

The Ninth Circuit reversed the case against the chief on an evidentiary mistake, but implied that the punitives awarded were reasonable and justifiable.

Green v Butler, 420 F3d 689 (2005)
Parole agents entered Green's home without knocking and announcing. Green was renting a room to a parolee. The officers saw Green in his garage, walked past him and into the house.

The Seventh Circuit Court of Appeals ruled that agents/police must knock and announce before entering premises. Therefore, the agents could not be granted summary judgment. The court also said that any agent or officer should know this, and, therefore, qualified immunity was not available.

VI. Interrogations

A citizen who has his Fifth, Sixth, or Fourteenth Amendment rights violated by an unconstitutional interrogation may sue the officers who violate those rights. Chapter 8, on statements, reflects the constitutional issues officers need to know to avoid violating a citizen's Fifth, Sixth, or Fourteenth Amendment rights.

Obviously, as a practical matter, the vast majority of sustainable civil rights suits will be brought by citizens whose Fourteenth Amendment due process rights have been violated. On the other hand, it is presently very difficult to bring suit simply because officers failed to comply with a MIRANDA technicality [e.g. Enoch v Gramley, 70 F3d 1490, 1496 (7th Cir 1995)].

Fourteenth Amendment violations

Officers may be sued when they violate a suspect's Fourteenth Amendment rights. This occurs usually when the officers overbear the suspect's will.

Cooper v Dupnik, 963 F3d 1220 (1992)
Officers thought Cooper committed a serious crime. Officers took Cooper into custody and gave him his rights. Cooper asserted them. The officers continued to question Cooper in order to rebut a possible defense and to keep him off of the witness stand (i.e. if Cooper took the witness stand, the officers thought that Cooper could be impeached with his statement, even though it was elicited in violation of his Fifth Amendment rights). The officers held Cooper incommunicado for about 24 hours before realizing that he did not commit the crime. During that period the officers used, according to the court, "sophisticated psychological torture" to try to get a confession. Cooper later sued under Section 1983.

The Ninth Circuit Court of Appeals ruled that the officers' conduct violated the Fourteenth Amendment. Therefore, the officers' motion for summary judgment was denied.

Since the law was clearly established at the time of the violation, the officers were not permitted to avail themselves of the qualified immunity doctrine.

Fifth Amendment violations

Officers may be sued when they violate a suspect's Fifth Amendment rights. This occurs usually when officers either don't warn suspects in custody or fail to cease questioning when a suspect asserts his right to silence and/or an attorney.

However, a statement obtained in violation of a suspect's Fifth Amendment rights that is to be used only outside the criminal arena (civil, disciplinary, etc.) cannot be the subject of a Section 1983 suit.

CHAVEZ V MARTINEZ, 123 S Ct 1994 (2003)
An officer shot Martinez. The officer's sergeant rode with Martinez to the hospital and took a statement from Martinez, even though Martinez told the officer that he (Martinez) didn't want to talk. The sergeant needed the statement for administrative purposes.

Later, Martinez sued the sergeant for violating his Fifth Amendment rights.

The United States Supreme Court ruled that a person cannot sue under Section 1983 for violation of his Miranda rights unless a criminal charge is filed and the statement used as part of the criminal process. Therefore, the complaint was thrown out.

Hanson v Dane County, 608 F3d 335 (7th Cir 2010)
Someone called 911 and hung up. The dispatcher called back, but no one answered. Officers went to the home, but the female who called could not remember why she called. The officers entered to make sure everyone was okay and questioned the residents even though the residents asked the officers to leave.

The Seventh Circuit Court of Appeals ruled that it was reasonable for officers to enter under these circumstances and ask questions of everyone until it could be established whether or not a crime had been committed. Although Hanson was in custody, the answers he gave were never used in court. Therefore, the officers were given summary judgment by the court.

Sornberger v City of Knoxville, 434 F3d 1006 (2006)
A guy robbed a bank. A bank employee who viewed the robbery on video commented that the robber looked a lot like Sornberger, who had previously had an account at the bank. Sornberger was in financial trouble at the time, so he became a prime suspect.

When the employee looked at the video pictures of the robber from a different angle, he noticed there "was less of the likeness." In fact, at certain angles, the robber did not look like Sornberger. The camera footage itself lacked clarity of resolution, so it was hard to make out detail.

An eyewitness to the robbery said the perpetrator was 5'9," about 160 pounds, dark complected, clean shaven, and in his 30s. Sornberger was 5'11," had blond hair, blue eyes, a fair complexion, and a mustache.

Neither the US Attorney nor the state's attorney would authorize an arrest warrant.

The officers picked up both Mr. and Mrs. Sornberger and brought them to the station. Initially both presented identical alibis; they were on the computer at his parents' home. Mrs. Sornberger later confessed to their involvement in the armed robbery. At the suppression hearing, the judge found her confession to be voluntary and in compliance with MIRANDA.

Shortly thereafter, a serial armed robber confessed to many robberies, including the one at the bank in question. Officers sent a picture of Sornberger's ear to the FBI to compare it to the bank robber's ear. The

FBI concluded that the two ears were different, thereby corroborating the fact that he did not commit the robbery.

The case against the Sornbergers was dismissed, and the Sornbergers sued under Section 1983.

The Federal District Court granted summary judgment in favor of the officers.

The Seventh Circuit ruled that a "reasonable jury certainly could find that probable cause did not exist." Therefore, "a determination of probable cause at the summary judgment stage was improper." The court also ruled that qualified immunity was not available to the officers, as the officers misrepresented the facts to the state's attorney when they finally obtained a search warrant for the computer Sornberger was using.

As to Mrs. Sornberger (Theresa), the Seventh Circuit ruled that the officers who took Theresa to the station could not avail themselves of qualified immunity. Theresa testified that she voluntarily went to the station, but she said that was in response to the officers' statement that she "needed" to accompany them to the station.

At the station, she was told that she had been seen at the bank at the time of the robbery (which was a lie), and she was told that her children might be taken from her. So even though she sat in the front seat of the police car and was not handcuffed in any way, the court held that it was a question for the jury as to whether she was restrained in a significant way. Finally, Theresa alleged that the officers never gave her Miranda warnings. The police contended that they did.

The court ruled that, even though a court had already ruled that she had been given her rights, she could re-litigate that before the jury as a Section 1983 violation.

California Attorneys for Criminal Justice v Butts, 195 F3d 1039 (1999)
Officers, when interrogating suspects, failed to honor scrupulously the suspect's right to cut off questioning by continuing to question the suspect after the suspect had asked for an attorney or asserted his right to silence.

The plaintiff successfully sued Butts, the Chief of Police and the City of Santa Monica; and the Ninth Circuit affirmed. The United States Supreme Court refused to hear the appeal.

> *Again, an area of increasing vulnerability within the civil arena for officers is the age-old tendency of officers to pick up a suspect on reasonable suspicion and bring him down to the station for questioning. This is, of course, a violation of the suspect's Fourth Amendment rights which can result in a civil suit* [*see* DUNAWAY V NEW YORK, 442 US 200 (1979)].

Cooper v Dupnik, 963 F3d 1220 (1992)
Officers thought Cooper committed a serious crime. Officers took him into custody and gave him his rights. Cooper asserted them. The officers continued to question Cooper in order to rebut a possible defense and to keep him off of the witness stand (i.e. if Cooper took the witness stand, the officers thought that Cooper could be impeached with his statement even though it was elicited in violation of his Fifth Amendment rights). Cooper later sued under Section 1983. The officers held Cooper incommunicado for about 24 hours before realizing that he did not commit the crime.

The Ninth Circuit ruled that the plaintiff's facts supported a cause of action for a Fifth Amendment violation. Therefore, summary judgment was not appropriate, and the officers' motion was denied.

Since the law was clearly established at the time of the violation, the officers were not permitted to avail themselves of the qualified immunity doctrine.

Aleman v Hanover Park, 662 F3d 897 (2011)
Aleman was brought to the station for questioning on suspicion that he shook a baby, and the baby died. Aleman was at the station for about an hour, and he had not yet been questioned. Aleman asked to leave. An officer told him he couldn't leave; that he was under arrest.

Aleman asked to call his attorney. The officer said he could. Aleman's attorney told the officer over the phone that the officer could not talk to his client—that the attorney was invoking the client's rights.

After hanging up, the officer asked Aleman if he wanted to talk. Aleman told the officer that the attorney had warned Aleman not to talk. Aleman also asked again to go home. The officer then said, "If I don't get to talk to you, you're not going home."

Aleman again called his lawyer, and the lawyer apparently told Aleman that Aleman could talk to the officers. Aleman then "confessed" and was charged.

The Seventh Circuit Court of Appeals ruled that when a suspect asks to speak to his attorney, an officer must cut off questioning him and may not reinitiate questioning (for at least two weeks if the suspect is in custody). That is true even if and after the suspect talks to his attorney. (See MINNICK V MISSISSIPPI.) Therefore, the officer(s) were not given qualified immunity for the violation.

Also, the officer(s) lied to Aleman about the results of the medical exam of the victim, and later it was determined that Aleman did not kill the baby.

VII. Conspiracies to Violate Constitutional Rights

Title 42 U.S.C. Section 1985 provides additional recourse to citizens who have been deprived of their constitutional rights as a result of "conspiracies" between two or more officers.

The statute

The statute states in pertinent part: "If two or more persons in any State or Territory conspire, or go in disguise on the highway or in the premises of another, for the purpose of depriving, either directly or indirectly, any person or class of persons of the equal protection of the laws... in any case of conspiracy set forth in this section, if one or more persons engage therein do, or cause to be done, any act in furtherance of the object of such conspiracy, whereby another individual is injured in his person or property, or deprived of having and exercising any right or privilege of a citizen of the United States, the party so injured or deprived may have an action for the recovery of damages, occasioned by such injury or deprivation, against any one or more of the conspirators."

Failure to act

Officers must understand that under Section 1985 they can be subjected to civil liability, not only as a result of their involvement in overt acts in furtherance of the conspiracy, but also may be subjected to liability as a result of their failure to act. For example, many successful suits are now being brought against officers who do not actively participate but who fail to intervene when present during an ongoing civil rights violation.

Hypothetical
Officers stop a motorist on a traffic violation. During the stop, one officer brutalizes the driver while the other officer makes no attempt to stop or restrain his fellow officer from the excessive force administered. The driver sues both officers and wins. The passive officer lost because he failed to intervene.

VIII. Liability of Governmental Units

Official policy or custom

Municipalities and other local governmental units may be held liable under Section 1983 if the unconstitutional conduct was the result of departmental policy or custom.

In MONELL V NEW YORK CITY the United States Supreme Court explained: "Local governing bodies, therefore, can be sued directly in Section 1983 for monetary, declaratory, or injunction relief where, as here, the action that is alleged to be unconstitutional implements or executes a policy statement, ordinance, regulation, or decision officially adopted and promulgated by that body's officers. Moreover, although the touchstone of the Section 1983 action against a government body is an allegation that official policy is responsible for a deprivation of rights protected by the Constitution, local governments, like every other Section 1983 'person,' by the very terms of the statute, may be sued for constitutional deprivations visited pursuant to governmental 'custom' even though such a custom has not received formal approval through the body's official decision-making channels... Although not authorized by written law, such practices of state officials could well be so permanent and well settled as to constitute a custom or usage with the force of law" [436 US 658 (1978)].

Rationale for municipal liability

The United States Supreme Court has also explained the rationale for the expanding liability of municipalities: "The knowledge that a municipality will be liable for all of its injurious conduct, whether committed in good faith or not, should create an incentive for officials who may harbor doubts about the lawfulness of their intended actions to err on the side of protecting citizens' constitutional rights. Furthermore, the threat that damages might be levied against the city may encourage those in a policy-making position to institute internal rules and programs designed to minimize the likelihood of unintentional infringements on constitutional rights" [OWEN V CITY OF INDEPENDENCE, MO, 445 US 622 (1980)].

Didzerekis v Stewart, 41 F Supp 2d 840 (1999)

Stewart was mentally ill, violent, and had attempted previously to kill his wife and himself.

One evening, Stewart's wife called 911 requesting emergency help. Officers arrived at 8:35 p.m. but did not enter until 9:20 p.m. During that period, Stewart killed his wife. The plaintiff alleged that the officers were familiar with the continual and continuous problems at the victim's home and did not respond to them as quickly. Also, there was some evidence that the officers needed to set up some kind of perimeter.

The wife's administrator sued under Section 1983.

The Seventh Circuit Court of Appeals ruled that the plaintiff had stated a MONELL claim in the complaint and that the City of Naperville could not be relieved of responsibility through summary judgment.

Fittano v Klein, 788 F Supp 1451 (ND IL 1992)

A 5-year-old neighbor of Fittano's, Kristina, visited John Fittano's daughter. The next day Kristina told her school teacher that John Fittano had "touched her private parts" in the bathroom of Fittano's home. Kristina also said that Fittano had molested his own daughter. Kristina was interviewed four or five times. During one interview Kristina alleged that there was blood, urine, the devil, death threats, the presence of other men, etc. Each interview contained varied descriptions of what occurred. Based solely on these interviews and the recommendation of the Advocacy Center, an officer arrested Fittano. Fittano consented to the search of his home, but no evidence was found. Later, the grounds for the arrest were determined to be frivolous. (It is hard to determine from the opinion, but apparently during the period when Kristina was at Fittano's home, John Fittano was at a Chicago Bears football game.)

As a result of the arrest, etc., Fittano was deprived of seeing his own daughter for two years and was otherwise deprived of his constitutional rights.

The Seventh Circuit Court of Appeals ruled that the arresting officer could not avail himself of summary judgment or qualified immunity. Furthermore, the court held that the city itself may be liable for "referring investigation of certain classes of criminal activity to an untrained group—the Advocacy Center." The court further stated: "If the Village failed to train its police officers in the proper procedure for handling referrals and arrests in sexual abuse cases, such that its failure to train may be found to amount to deliberate indifference to the plaintiff's rights, the village may be liable under Section 1983." The village's motion to dismiss was therefore also denied.

Fairley v Luman, 281 F3d 913 (2002)
Officers had a warrant for John Fairley's twin brother. The officers arrested John, and kept him in custody for twelve days, despite his protestations.

A jury exonerated the officers involved but found the city liable and awarded the plaintiff $11,250. The district court awarded attorney's fees of $92,211.83.

The city appealed.

The Ninth Circuit ruled that the city's warrant procedures followed a policy or custom of inaction about the problem of picking up the wrong person on a warrant. Therefore, the court affirmed the decision of the district court.

Sornberger v City of Knoxville, 434 F3d 1006 (2006)
Someone robbed a bank. A bank employee who viewed the robbery on video commented that the robber looked a lot like Sornberger, who had previously had an account at the bank. Sornberger was in financial trouble at the time, so he became a prime suspect.

When the employee looked at the video pictures of the robber from a different angle, he noticed there "was less of the likeness." In fact, at certain angles, the robber did not look like Sornberger. The camera footage itself lacked clarity of resolution, so it was hard to make out detail.

An eyewitness to the robbery said the perpetrator was 5'9," about 160 pounds, dark complected, clean shaven, and in his 30s. Sornberger was 5'11," had blond hair, blue eyes, a fair complexion, and a mustache.

Neither the US Attorney nor the state's attorney would authorize an arrest warrant.

The officers picked up both Mr. and Mrs. Sornberger and brought them to the station. Initially both presented identical alibis; they were on the computer at his parents' home. Mrs. Sornberger later confessed to their involvement in the armed robbery. At the suppression hearing, the judge found her confession to be voluntary and in compliance with MIRANDA.

Shortly thereafter, a serial armed robber confessed to many robberies, including the one at the bank in question.

Officers sent a picture of Sornberger's ear to the FBI to compare it to the bank robber's ear. The FBI concluded that the two ears were different, thereby corroborating the fact that he did not commit the robbery.

The case against the Sornbergers was dismissed, and the Sornbergers sued under Section 1983.

The Federal District Court granted summary judgment in favor of the officers.

The Seventh Circuit ruled that a "reasonable jury certainly could find that probable cause did not exist." Therefore, "a determination of probable cause at the summary judgment stage was improper." The court also ruled that qualified immunity was not available to the officers, as the officers misrepresented the facts to the states attorney when they finally obtained a search warrant for the computer Sornberger was using.

As to Mrs. Sornberger (Theresa), the Seventh Circuit ruled that the officers who took Theresa to the station could not avail themselves of qualified immunity. Theresa testified that she voluntarily went to the station, but she said that was in response to the officers' statement that she "needed" to accompany them to the station. At the station, she was told that she had been seen at the bank at the time of the robbery (which was a lie), and she was told that her children might be taken from her. So even though she sat in the front seat of the police car and was not handcuffed in any way, the court held that it was a question for the jury as to whether she was restrained in a significant way.

Finally, the court ruled that the city of Knoxville could be liable for the "policy" of telling women that they could lose their children if the women did not confess.

Wall v County of Orange, 364 F3d 1107 (2004)
Wall, a dentist, took his Lexis SUV to a car wash for an oil change and wash. The son of the owner of the car wash, Chala, was working the desk and asked Wall for his address and phone number. Wall did not want to provide that information, but Chala insisted that it was "store policy" that all customers provide the information. Wall finally asked for the return of his car. Chala refused, stating that the car was already being worked on and that it could not be returned. Wall went back to the service area, and Chala told him that he was not to go back to the service area. Finally the police were called. Wall was angry and spoke angrily to the officer about what had happened.

The officer handcuffed Wall, arrested him for obstructing, resisting, and trespassing. The officer forced Wall face first into the patrol car. Because of injuries sustained, Wall could no longer practice dentistry. All of the charges against Wall were later dismissed.

Wall sued for false arrest and false imprisonment under Section 1983.

The above facts were sufficient to support an action against the officer and the department. Therefore, an award of summary judgment and qualified immunity were not appropriate in this case.

Arpin v Santa Clara Valley, 261 F3d 912 (1998)
Arpin was arrested on a minor offense and sued the sheriff because she was strip-searched unconstitutionality since there was no reasonable suspicion that she was concealing contraband, etc. Arpin could not prove that the sheriff had a policy, practice, pattern, or custom of strip-searching arrestees who committed minor offenses.

The district court and the Ninth Circuit Court of Appeals ruled that summary judgment in favor of the Sheriff was granted.

Watts v County of Sacramento, 136 Cal App3d 232 (1982)
Officers had an arrest warrant for Chris Burgess. They received an anonymous tip that Burgess was living at a certain address. The officers went to that address and knocked on the door. Chris Pryor answered the

door. When the officer asked the resident if his name was "Chris" and the resident said, "Yes," the officer arrested him and detained the others in the home. Burgess was not there. The residents at the house sued the county.

The district court granted summary judgment for the officers and the department, but the Ninth Circuit reversed stating that the plaintiffs could possibly prove that this was a custom or practice of the department.

Lukse v County of Los Angeles, 286 F3d 906 (1998)
Officers of the LA Sheriff's Office were required to carry their weapons at all times. During a five-year period, the department experienced eighty incidents of officers brandishing or discharging weapons off duty. During fifteen of those incidents the officers were drinking. The department knew about these incidents, but did little about them or took any steps to ensure that the incidents would not occur in the future.

An LA Sheriff's Deputy, Kirsch, while drinking one evening at a bar, managed to drink his way up to a .25 BAC while arguing with Huffman, another drunk at the bar. To end the argument, Kirsch shot and killed Huffman.

Huffman's estate sued the officer and the Department under Section 1983. An expert witness for the estate testified that the Department had devoted insufficient attention to the unlawful use of firearms by deputies, and that the department had not dealt with the issue of guns and alcohol.

The Ninth Circuit ruled that the county had not been shown to have acted with deliberate indifference to the plaintiff. Case dismissed.

Chew v Gates, 27 F3d 1432 (1994)
Officers stopped Chew on a traffic offense, but Chew ran off into a scrap yard. The officers determined that Chew had three felony warrants. Officers warned Chew to surrender or the officers would send their "chew" dog after him. The dog, a German Sheppard, actually named Volker had been taught to bite the suspect and drag him. Since Chew was hidden the dog continued to bite and drag Chew until the handler, Bunch, arrived.

The City conceded that all dogs are taught to attack and seize people who are concealed—whether they resist or not and whether they are violent or not.

Chew also alleged that he surrendered and that Officer Bunch ordered the dog to attack Chew even after he gave up. The officers said that Chew refused to surrender and had hit the dog with a pipe. The officer admitted that he kicked Chew.

The district court granted summary judgment to the defendants except Bunch. The jury rendered a verdict and damages against Bunch.

The Ninth Circuit Court of Appeals ruled that in addition to Bunch's liability, the city could be liable if the city teaches and has an unconstitutional policy related to dogs biting and seizing all suspects. (The record showed that dogs inflicted injury in 40% of the cases where they were used.)

Also, the city could be liable under the theory of deliberate indifference if the city had no policy related to the handling of dogs or left the handling up to the discretion of the handlers.

Liability of supervisors and vicarious liability

Complainants who believe that an officer has violated their constitutional rights will often sue the officer's supervisor. In order to sue a supervisor successfully a plaintiff must prove that the supervisor's act or omission caused the plaintiff's damage or injury. In other words, there must be some personal responsibility by the supervisor [Duncan v Duckworth, 644 F2d 653 A (1981)].

Simple negligence by a supervisor is usually not sufficient to support a case under Section 1983. Usually gross negligence or indifference is required to state a cause of action [Hinshaw v Doffer, 785 F2d 1260 (1986)].

Many of the successful suits result when plaintiffs prove that the supervisors or the department was told or was aware that they were doing something wrong and did not correct it. A classic example in this area is training in constitutional criminal procedure which is almost universally deficient. A supervisor does not have to be directly involved. It is enough that there is a link between the act or omission and the acquiescence of the supervisor [Stringer v City of Chicago, 464 F Supp 887 (1979)].

IX. Failure to Train

Failure to train officers adequately in the area of constitutional criminal procedure can result in civil liability for a city or other governing body [CITY OF CANTON V HARRIS, 489 US 378 (1989)].

The standard for determining liability is "deliberate indifference" to the issue.

According to the Supreme Court, an example would be if a department failed to teach the constitutional limitations related to TENNESSEE V GARNER, 471 US 1 (1985)

A second example raised by the Supreme Court would be a situation in which the department failed to train where "that need for further training must have been plainly obvious to the city policy makers who, nevertheless, are deliberately indifferent to the need." This might be training in the area of TERRY and traffic stops, where the laws are well developed and officers often make mistakes, but it can arise in any constitutional context.

> **Fittano v Klein, 788 F Supp 1451 (ND IL 1992)**
> A five-year-old neighbor of Fittano's, Kristina, visited John Fittano's daughter. The next day Kristina told her school teacher that John Fittano had "touched her private parts" in the bathroom of Fittano's home. Kristina also said that Fittano had molested his own daughter. Kristina was interviewed four or five times. During one interview Kristina alleged that there was blood, urine, the devil, death threats, the presence of other men, etc. Each interview contained varied descriptions of what occurred. Based solely on these interviews and the recommendation of the Advocacy Center, an officer arrested Fittano. Fittano consented to the search of his home, but no evidence was found. Later, the grounds for the arrest were determined to be frivolous. (It is hard to determine from the opinion, but apparently during the period when Kristina was at Fittano's home, John Fittano was at a Chicago Bears football game.)
>
> As a result, Fittano was deprived of seeing his own daughter for two years and was otherwise deprived of his constitutional rights.
>
> The Seventh Circuit Court of Appeals ruled that the arresting officer could not avail himself of summary judgment or qualified immunity. Furthermore the court held that the city itself may be liable for "referring investigation of certain classes of criminal activity to an untrained group—the Advocacy Center." The court further stated that "if the Village failed to train its police officers in the proper procedure for handling referrals and arrests in sexual abuse cases, such that its failure to train may be found to amount to deliberate indifference to the plaintiff's rights, the village may be liable under Section 1983." The village's motion to dismiss was therefore also denied.

Munger v Glasgow, PD, 227 F3d 1082 (2000)
Officers responded to a problem drunk in a bar. The officers removed the drunk, Munger, from the bar. It was very cold out and Munger only had a t-shirt on. The officers told Munger not to drive his truck, so Munger wandered off. The next day he was found a couple blocks away, dead.

The Ninth Circuit ruled that the officers had put Munger in danger through some affirmative conduct. Therefore, the officers were denied qualified immunity.

The Ninth Circuit further refused to grant summary judgment for the police department, in that the plaintiffs may be able to prove a deliberate indifference in their training of officers in dealing with drunks, particularly in bad situations (for example, on cold nights).

Hopkins v Andaya, 958 F2d 881 (1992)
Officer Andaya was called to Capri Hotel in response to Hopkins who was causing a disturbance and threatening to "shoot the place up." The officer determined that Hopkins was unarmed and not a danger to anyone, so he released Hopkins. Hopkins then began to bray or howl at a traffic light. When the guy started to walk back toward the hotel, Andaya decided to stop him.

During the confrontation, Andaya said that Hopkins took Andaya's baton away and started to hit him (the officer) on the head and shoulders. Andaya then shot the guy six times. Apparently during this period also, Hopkins (after being shot) chased the officer across the street, where the officer shot him four more times.

A witness, however, stated that Hopkins never had Andaya's baton and that as soon as Andaya fell, he shot Hopkins. No warning was ever given. The witness further stated that Andaya was on his feet when he fired the last the shot. Hopkins died.

The district court awarded summary judgment, but the Ninth Circuit Court of Appeals reversed, stating that Andaya's hospital records tended to show that he was not hit (by Hopkins) where he said he was and that the witness' statement appeared to be more accurate than Andaya's. The court deduced that, if Hopkins had been shot five times and Anaya was on his feet for the last shot, a jury could conclude that the force exhibited was excessive. In fact, there was evidence that the officer may have shot four times after Hopkins was wounded and incapacitated to a great extent.

Finally, the Ninth Circuit ruled that summary judgment for the city and the chief were inappropriate in this case as "the police chief and the city might be held liable for improper training or improper procedure even if Andaya is exonerated, since as the court stated, 'They put an officer on the street who is so badly trained and instructed he lets his baton be taken away from him and then has to kill an unarmed civilian to save his own life.' Andaya has a history of citizen complaints of excessive force, a reputation for being quick-tempered, and has drawn or fired his gun inappropriately several times before. These facts certainly bear on whether the city properly trained Andaya, and whether they should have sent him out on the streets carrying a weapon."

Ross v Austin, 343 F3d 915 (2003)
A small-town officer saw Miller in a parking lot right after Miller had attempted to shoot his wife. The officer was within twelve feet of Miller, he pointed a shotgun at Miller, and told Miller to drop his weapon. Miller had his weapon raised and pointed at the officer. He also told the 15 bystanders to get down. The officer took a position behind a truck. Miller ran into a liquor store and took the manager hostage. Miller then demanded to talk to his wife. When his wife was located by phone, Miller spoke briefly to her and then he shot and killed the manager and himself.

The manager's wife sued under Section 1983 alleging that, had the officer undergone hostage training and other training related to this situation, her husband would be alive. Also, the department's chief had never attended mandatory training that taught how to handle these situations. The wife alleged that had the officer attended a class in how to deal with these problems: he would have worn his bullet-proof vest, he would have used a different weapon, he would have shot Miller, he would not have allowed Miller to enter the liquor store, he would not have allowed Miller to contact his wife (thereby avoiding further agitation), and he would have taken other measures that would not have resulted in endangering the manager's life.

The Seventh Circuit Court of Appeals ruled that the officers of this small town could not be held to the same training standards of larger cities. The court held that the department did not show a deliberate indifference to training. The court therefore held that summary judgment in favor of the defendants was appropriate.

United States v Proano, 912 F3d 431 (2019)
Officers stopped a car on an apparent traffic violation. The driver got out and ran away. The driver did not put the car in park when he ran away, and the car continued to move toward the police car. The suspect car ultimately became stuck between two cars. There was one passenger in the front passenger seat and four or five in the back seat. The officer present told the occupants to stay in the car. Apparently, they did.

Chicago police officer, Proano, and another officer arrived soon afterward as a backup.

A backseat passenger reached over the front seat and hit the gas pedal but the car did not move. Finally, the suspect car broke free and began to move in reverse. There was apparently no one in its path. Proano shot into the car and bullets hit one occupant's shoulder and another bullet hit a different occupant's leg and foot.

The US Attorney indicted Proano for violating the passengers' rights by using excessive force, i.e. a violation of the passengers' Fourth Amendment rights.

Both the prosecution and Proano were allowed to use the CPD policies, procedures, and training "to prove or disprove that Proano acted <u>willfully</u>." In other words, if Proano could show that he was just following his training, it might impact the jury's decision as to the willfulness of his conduct. On the other hand, if the prosecution could prove that Chicago officers are told not to shoot in these situations, it would reflect that Proano's conduct was willful in violation of the statute he was being prosecuted under. (Apparently, the jury thought the conduct was willful.)

The district court judge gave the following jury instruction at the end of the trial:

> "You have heard evidence about <u>training</u> the defendant received relating to the use of deadly force. <u>You should not consider this training when you decide whether the defendant's use of force was reasonable or unreasonable.</u> But you may consider the training when you decide what the defendant intended at the time he acted." (emphasis added)

The jury convicted Proano on both counts.

The Seventh Circuit ruled that the testimony of the training officers about the training given officers about use of force was admissible to prove Proano's state of mind (even though the training officers could not say for sure that Proano was in their classes).

X. Attorneys' Fees

The factor that drives many constitutional tort suits and the reason for the dramatic increase in the number of claims and cases filed under 1983 is that attorneys who "win" for their clients get attorney's fees under Title 42 U.S.C. Section 1988.

In a recent case, for example, the attorney obtained a settlement for his client of $1,000. The attorney received $459,000 as an attorney's fee.

The judge's discretion

Section 1988 provides that a trial court in its discretion may award attorneys' fees to the prevailing party in a civil rights action [42 U.S.C. Section 1988 (b)].

The rationale for Section 1988

Section 1988 was enacted to help vindicate the rights of a citizen, even if the officers' unconstitutional conduct did not cause great injury or damage. Obviously most citizens cannot afford attorneys, and if the injury or damage is minor, no attorney would take the case on contingency because the attorney could never make enough money on the suit to make the case worth his/her effort. "The overriding goal of Section 1988 is to reimburse, with a reasonable attorney's fee, those private attorneys general who invoke and thereby invigorate federal constitutional and statutory rights" [Herbst v Ryan, 90 F3d 1300 (1996)].

Factors in the determination of attorneys' fees

The United States Supreme Court in HENSLEY V ECKERHART, 461 US 424 (1983), gave some guidance to lower courts in the determination of attorneys' fees. Relevant to the discussion are:

1. Time and labor required
2. The novelty and difficulty of the questions
3. The skill required to perform the legal service
4. Opportunity costs for taking the case
5. The attorney's customary fee
6. Whether the fee is fixed or contingent
7. Time limitations imposed by the client or the circumstances
8. The amount involved and results obtained
9. The experience, reputation, and ability of the attorneys
10. The undesirability of the case
11. The nature and length of the professional relationship with the client
12. Awards in similar cases

Application of the factors

In CITY OF RIVERSIDE V RIVERA, 477 US 561 (1986), the plaintiffs were awarded only $33,350. The judge awarded attorneys' fees of $245,456.25.

The Supreme Court upheld the award in part because the attorneys vindicated important constitutional rights that cannot be valued solely in monetary terms.

Attorneys' fees when the jury awards a nominal amount

The United States Supreme Court has emphasized that, where the real purpose of the suit is not to vindicate a constitutional right but to make money for the plaintiff's lawyer, the trial court may reduce the attorney's fees.

FARRAR V HOBBY, 506 US 103 (1992)
The plaintiff sued for $17,000,000 but received only $1.00. The trial judge refused to award "reasonable" attorney's fees.

The United States Supreme Court upheld the nominal award of attorney's fees, because the attorney did not vindicate anyone's rights.

Attorneys' fees when the case settles
If the case settles, attorneys' fees are normally not appropriate as there is no "prevailing party."

Petersen v Gibson, 372 F2d 862 (2004)
Petersen got her hair colored at a salon. The stylist botched the job twice. On the third try, Petersen was apparently under a hair dryer when her stylist went to lunch and forgot about her. Petersen then left the salon in a huff without paying. The salon called the police. An officer tried to mediate the argument, but Petersen was only willing to pay part of the bill and the salon would only accept full payment. The officer arrested Petersen.

The salon pressed the prosecution for seven months, but finally the state dropped the case.

Petersen sued the salon and the officer and won. Later, the officer settled the suit (for $10,000), and attorney's fees of $288,087.25 were assessed against Gibson along with court costs.

The Seventh Circuit Court of Appeals ruled that if the case is settled there is no prevailing party, and, therefore, the lower court's ruling on fees was reversed.

This is going to be a huge incentive for departments to settle.

Awards to Defendants
When officers win, they are obviously the prevailing party and deserve attorneys' fees. As a practical matter, however, a plaintiff is generally judgment proof. Even when they are not, judges are reluctant to award the state attorneys' fees unless the plaintiff's claim was frivolous.

XI. Defenses to 1983 Actions

Generally, once the plaintiff has stated a claim upon which relief can be granted, the defendant's main defense is qualified immunity.

Stating a claim
First, the plaintiff must claim that the defendant violated a constitutional right of the plaintiff [BAKER V MCCOLLAN, 443 US 137 (1970)].

Qualified immunity: good faith
The state and its officers once had absolute immunity from civil suits. That is no longer the case. However, officers may have qualified immunity, or rely on a "good faith" type defense, even when their conduct violates a citizen's constitutional rights.

"Officials who perform discretionary functions are afforded 'qualified immunity' shielding them from civil damages liability as long as their actions could reasonably have been thought consistent with the rights they are alleged to have violated" [Anderson v Creighton, 483 US 635 (1987); Harris v Roderick, 126 F2d 1189 (1997)].

The difference between good faith and qualified immunity

The good faith doctrine as explained in Chapter 6, on miscellaneous search and seizure issues, states that if there is a constitutional violation, the state is required to prove that the officers reasonably relied on a statute, an ordinance, a court order or case law to support the search or seizure or other constitutional intrusion.

Qualified immunity is invoked by the officer when he/she violates a suspect's/citizen's rights, and the officer reasonably did not know what the rule was because it (the rule) had not yet been specifically defined by the courts or the legislature. It is not required that a case(s) be exactly on point or that the rule has been specifically stated or be exactly on all fours with the facts at bar.

But it is up to/the burden of the plaintiff to prove that there was a case or rule that the officer should have known in order to defeat an officer's motion for qualified immunity.

Escobedo v Bender, 600 F3d 770 (7th Cir 2010)

Escobedo was suicidal. He had a gun and said he didn't want to hurt anyone and that he desperately wanted to talk to someone about his drug addiction and life circumstances. A negotiator talked to Escobedo. The deputy chief decided to use tear gas because negotiations appeared to be going nowhere, pedestrian and vehicle traffic was increasing, and Escobedo was apparently beginning to barricade himself in. The deputy chief apparently testified that he wasn't aware that Escobedo had said that he didn't want to hurt anybody, including police.

The police then swarmed Escobedo's residence while setting off tear gas and flash bang grenades. Escobedo then shot and killed himself.

Escobedo's estate brought suit under Section 1983.

The Seventh Circuit ruled that, although there was no Seventh Circuit case directly on point, officers knew, or should have known, that when a suspect does not present a threat to officers, the use of this much force cannot be justified under qualified immunity. Therefore, the motion for qualified immunity was denied.

Navarro v Barthel, 952 F2d 331 (1991)

A confidential (apparently) reliable informant told officers that Villa was dealing drugs out of his house and explained how he knew that. The informant said that "Villa's home was the second house on the right side of a driveway leading off Agate Road to the Southern Tallow Company." The police determined that Villa lived on the Tallow company's property, but could find out nothing else. The informant "evidently did not include the house on the corner when he described the house to be searched as the second house along the driveway." So the police searched the house of Navarro instead.

The Ninth Circuit Court of Appeals ruled that a jury should determine whether or not the officer's mistake was reasonable.

> *The court in making this ruling relied on the case of* Maryland v Garrison, *a "good faith" case where the officers serving a warrant accidentally searched the wrong premises.*

What happens when qualified immunity is denied?

If summary judgment based on qualified immunity is denied, the issue is simply left for the jury to decide [Thompson v Mahre, 110 F3d 716 (1997)].

When should the issue be raised?
Furthermore, the United States Supreme Court has explained to lower courts that the qualified immunity issue should be resolved early in the process.

Cases where officers were granted qualified immunity

Below are just a few cases where qualified immunity was granted. The issue is discussed many times throughout this chapter.

CITY OF ESCONDIDO V EMMONS, 139 S Ct 500 (2019)
Officers were called to a domestic problem for the second time in several weeks. Apparently, Trina was talking on the phone to her daughter when her daughter screamed for help. The call then disconnected. Trina then called 911.

Police were informed by dispatch that no one was answering the phone at the suspect apartment and that two children could be in the residence. The officers who arrived knocked on the door but could get no response. The officers tried to gain entry by talking to residents through a window, but to no avail.

All of a sudden, a man, Emmons, walked out from the apartment. The officers told Emmons not to close the door. Emmons closed it anyway. Emmons then tried to walk past the officers, but the officers stopped him and quickly took him to the ground and handcuffed him. He was then officially arrested. Apparently, the man was not involved in the domestic problem in any way and did not live in the apartment. But the officers did not know that at the time.

Emmons sued the officers for excessive force under Section 1983.

The district court judge ruled that the officer who took Emmons to the ground and handcuffed him deserved qualified immunity as there was no previous case that would have put the officer on notice that he was violating Emmons' constitutional rights.

The Ninth Circuit ruled that the officer did not deserve qualified immunity, as every officer should know that the "right to be free of excessive force was clearly established at the time of the events in question."

The United States Supreme Court reversed the Ninth Circuit, ruling that there was no case on point that would have put the officer on notice that he was violating Emmons' rights by taking him to the ground. The Court stated, "the clearly established right must be defined with specificity." This means the "existing precedent [must] squarely govern the specific facts at issue..."

The Court said that the Ninth Circuit should have asked, "What clearly established law / case says an officer in this situation should not stop a person and take him to the ground," (rather than the general rule the Ninth Circuit pronounced—that every officer should know not to use excessive force).

WILSON V LAYNE, 119 S Ct 1692 (1999)
Officers allowed news media people to accompany them while the officers served an arrest warrant on Wilson at about 6:30 a.m. The officers went to Wilson's parents' home to serve the warrant. Wilson was not there but his parents were. His parents were in various degrees of undress and the media took many pictures.

The United States Supreme Court ruled that allowing the media to enter went beyond the scope of the warrant and was therefore unconstitutional. However, the court ruled that officers could not have been "expected to predict the future course of constitutional law." Therefore, the officers were not subject to damages under the qualified immunity statute.

Montville v Lewis, 87 F3d 900 (1996)
City building inspectors saw evidence of city code violations from outside of Montville's home. They knocked on the door, and the contractor answered the door. The inspectors asked to enter the home. The contractor agreed, and the inspectors entered and found evidence of other violations. Montville sued the inspectors for violation of her Fourth Amendment rights.

The court ruled that the inspectors were entitled to qualified immunity under the Fourth Amendment proposition that the inspectors reasonably believed that the contractor had the authority to consent to the search (even though he did not). Therefore, the suit was thrown out.

> *Officers would be held to a higher standard, as any officer would or should know to inquire further about the authority of such persons to consent. (A close case, though.)*

Thompson v Mahre, 110 F3d 716 (1997)
Officers decided to knock and announce but not to wait when they were serving a warrant at Deshetres' residence. Deshetres had a long record of arrest for drugs, assault, robbery, interference with officers, etc. Also, a truck was just leaving the Deshetres residence as the officers arrived. The officers thought the people in the truck might notify Deshetres. The officers entered and engaged in a gun battle where people were hurt. Deshetres came out with a gun and was shot.

The district court ruled that the officers violated the plaintiff's rights and left to the jury the amount of damages. The jury decided that the sergeant who led the assault should be required to pay Deshetres $82,500 (for shooting him) and $10,000 to another resident who was frightened by the assault.

The Ninth Circuit Court of Appeals ruled that the officers reasonably believed that Deshetres would meet the officers with a weapon and would flush his drugs down the toilet. Therefore, the failure to wait was ostensibly reasonable. And the sergeant was entitled to qualified immunity as a matter of law.

Baker v Clover, 864 P2d 1069 (1993)
Baker drove up to his home on a residential street at 50 mph. The speed limit was 25 mph. An officer, Clover, who observed Baker did not activate his emergency equipment or try to stop Baker. Baker pulled into his driveway and then, after automatically opening his garage door, Baker drove into his garage. The officer wrote in his report, "I then approached the driver's door and shined my light inside." The driver opened the door, and the officer viewed a number of indications of intoxication, and, therefore, had probable cause to arrest for DUI.

The trial court ruled that the officer had entered the garage unconstitutionally. Therefore, Baker was awarded damages and attorney's fees.

The Arizona Court of Appeals ruled that an officer might not have been aware that a garage was protected by the Fourth Amendment in the circumstances encountered, because at that time in Arizona there was no case law or statute directly on point. Therefore, the officer was protected by qualified immunity, and the trial court's judgment was reversed.

Edwards v Cabrera, 58 F3d 290 (1996)
A bus driver called police stating that he thought he had seen a drug transaction at the Greyhound bus depot. The dispatcher did not give the driver's name. An officer went to the bus station and saw four black men standing together. The group disbanded when they saw the officer. The officer asked one of the men, Edwards, if she could speak to him. Edwards agreed and told the officer that he was there simply to drop off his brother. They went to Edwards' brother, who was already on the bus. His brother consented to a search of his luggage, and both Edwards and his brother were arrested. The prosecutor

refused to charge Edwards. Edwards sued the police for false imprisonment and the violation of his Fourth Amendment (seizure) rights.

The court ruled that the officers were protected by qualified immunity, in that it was not unreasonable for the officers to believe that they had probable cause to arrest Edwards under the circumstances. Therefore, Edwards did not have a viable Section 1983 claim.

Mendoza v Block, 27 F3d 1357 (1994)
Mendoza robbed a bank and escaped in a car. He then abandoned the car and fled on foot. He ran about a half mile and hid under some bushes on private property for several hours. The officers told Mendoza that he should come out or that they were going to send a dog/Rottweiler in after him. The dog caused some injury to Mendoza.

Mendoza brought a Section 1983 action claiming excessive force was used, in that the officers encouraged the dog to bite even after Mendoza surrendered, etc. The officers, of course, denied these allegations.

The Ninth Circuit ruled that the officers were protected by qualified immunity as Mendoza was dangerous to both the officers and nearby property owners. And Mendoza fought with the dog thereby increasing his pain.

> *The court noted that had there been evidence to show that the dog was permitted to bite Mendoza after he had surrendered, Mendoza would have had a cause of action and the officers would not have been allowed to claim qualified immunity.*

Cases where officers could not claim qualified immunity

Again, this book is loaded with lots of cases where qualified immunity was denied. The following are just a few cases where the courts have determined that the officer should have known that he was violating the suspect/citizens constitution rights. Therefore, qualified immunity was not available to remove him from the suit.

Harris v Roderick, 126 F2d 1189 (1997)
Officers went to serve an arrest warrant on a man, Randy Weaver, in his cabin/home. The officers got into a gun battle with a group of people in the house. One officer was killed and one person from the house was killed. The officers were then told by supervisory order to shoot any adult male with a weapon in the vicinity of the house. An officer shot a male, Harris, who had left the house and was running/trying to get back into it.

Harris sued for violation of Fourth Amendment rights. He said that there was no probable cause that he did anything wrong. The officers had no reason to believe that he was an immediate threat to anyone. Finally, the officers never warned Harris.

The Ninth Circuit Court of Appeals ruled that qualified immunity was not available for the shooter. Harris was not escaping, simply retreating into the cabin. Therefore, deadly force could not be used.

Ramierez v Butte Silver Bow County, 283 F3d 985 (2001)
An officer received two reports that the Ramierez household had a rocket launcher and other illegal weapons. The officer wrote up an affidavit and warrant but failed properly to fill in the blank that asked for the items to be searched for and seized. The officer then obtained a warrant and executed it. Nothing illegal was discovered.

Ramierez sued the officer for violations of his Fourth Amendment rights under Section 1983. The district court ruled that the officer enjoyed the protection of qualified immunity.

The Ninth Circuit ruled that the officer should have proofread the warrant. The court reversed and remanded the case for a determination by a jury as to whether a reasonable officer would have noticed the defects in the warrant.

Penilla v City of Huntington Park, 115 F3d 707 (1997)
Penilla became seriously ill while sitting on his porch. Officers arrived and found Penilla to be in need of medical services. They then broke into Penilla's home and deposited Penilla there. The next day Penilla's family members found Penilla dead.

Penilla's estate sued for Fourth and Fourteenth Amendment violations. The defendant officers moved to dismiss based on qualified immunity. The district court ruled that there was case law supporting the proposition that the officers had an affirmative duty to Penilla once they had begun the process and that there was no theory for entering Penilla's home.

The Ninth Circuit affirmed, ruling that the "officers in this case allegedly took affirmative actions that significantly increased the risk facing Penilla" and that there are lots of cases that stand for the proposition that if an officer exposes a person to danger, they are liable for the consequences. Therefore, qualified immunity was not appropriate, and the case was remanded for a jury trial.

Gibson v County of Washoe, 290 F3d 1175 (2002)
Gibson was a manic-depressive. He was going through a manic phase where he was acting weirdly at a convenience store. His wife reported that he had a loaded weapon with him and that he had just threatened to kill her. After Gibson was subdued, they took him to the jail. Officers found the pills to control his mental illness in Gibson's truck, and they gave them to the nurse in charge at the jail. Gibson acted violent, so the officers restrained him more and more and sprayed him with pepper spray. Gibson then had a heart attack and died.

The Ninth Circuit court of Appeals ruled that the officers who brought Gibson in had an affirmative duty to try to convey his medicine to responsible personnel, which they did. Therefore, they could not be held liable for Gibson's death, but the nurse could and so could the department.

Jenson v Oxnard, 145 F3d 1078 (1998)
An officer, while serving a search warrant, accidentally shot and killed his fellow officer, Jenson. Jenson's wife sued under Section 1983.

The Ninth Circuit ruled that the city and the officer involved could be liable under Section 1983. Therefore, qualified immunity was not appropriate.

Siebert v Severino, 256 F3d 648 (2001)
An officer received a call that horses at the Siebert farm were not provided with shelter or water. The officer went into the Sieberts' barn which was 60 feet from the house and was surrounded by a fence. The officer checked on the welfare of the horses and left a notice that the Sieberts had failed to provide adequate shelter and protection for the horses. Three days later, many officers returned and loaded up several horses in the trailer.

The district court granted summary judgment for the defendant/officer(s), but the Ninth Circuit Court of Appeals reversed ruling that the officer(s) violated the Fourth Amendment rights of the plaintiffs, Sieberts, by entering the barn and seizing the horses. The court further held that the laws in these areas were so well settled that the defendant, Severino, could not claim qualified immunity either for the unconstitutional search or seizure.

McNair v Coffey, 234 F3d 352 (2000)
Officers began to stop a traffic offender, McNair. McNair would not stop but drove on about a mile to a lighted area near a gas station. Since the area was "high crime" and the McNairs would not stop, eight squad cars were ultimately involved in the "high risk stop," and the officers pulled their weapons and used a loudspeaker to order the McNairs out the car. The driver was released after about an hour.

The McNairs sued. The jury awarded $5,000 to both Mr. and Mrs. McNair. The trial/district court set aside the jury verdict and award on qualified immunity grounds and entered judgment for the officers.

The Seventh Circuit Court of Appeals reversed, ruling that the officers in an excessive force situation can rarely avail themselves of qualified immunity. In this case the Seventh Circuit held that the officers were not protected by qualified immunity. The jury verdict was reinstated.

Clash v Beatty, 77 F3d 1045 (1996)
A witness told an officer that a child in a certain car in a parking lot had a gun and said, "If you don't get away from the car, I'm going to blow your weed off your head." Officers subsequently stopped the car and arrested the occupants. An officer shoved Clash into the squad car and Clash was injured. Later, it was determined that the gun was a cap gun. Clash sued under Section 1983 for excessive force.

The Seventh Circuit Court of Appeals ruled that the officer could not qualify for qualified immunity.

XII. Why Law Enforcement Is More Vulnerable

It is very obvious that the area of conduct which supports a cause of action by citizens is broadening. That is, almost all constitutional violations can now support a law suit. Furthermore, almost anyone within the law enforcement community can be successfully sued.

The courts have been increasing the areas of liability for many subtle, practical and legal reasons:

The courts hate the exclusionary rule and precedents are growing dramatically

Deep down, the courts want to deter officers from violating citizens' constitutional rights. But judges do not want to be blamed for throwing out perfectly good evidence against a guilty defendant.

So the most important subtle reason for enlarging the scope liability is that the courts hate the exclusionary rule because most courts realize that suppressing reliable evidence is unfair and almost always creates ill feelings among the citizenry. If the courts can permit citizens a broader base for civil suit, the courts feel more comfortable allowing evidence to be admitted, even when it technically should be suppressed if the rule were to be strictly enforced.

Finally, often when courts rule in cases, it becomes precedent that officers must know.

Government units have deep pockets

When officers violate a citizen's rights, the citizen would, as a practical matter, not be able to sue if the only parties the citizen could sue were the officers. Officers do not have enough money to satisfy most plaintiffs. The obvious choice for suit is the officers' department and the municipality or other employing agency.

Courts know that if the employing agency is liable, citizens will have a way to vindicate their rights, and the employing agency will tend to train their officers better.

The rights of guilty parties

Again, as a practical matter, citizens who are guilty of the crime have little chance of vindicating their rights. For instance, if a plaintiff was caught with a lot of dangerous drugs, a jury is simply not going to be very sympathetic about the plaintiff's rights being violated in the process.

The courts realize, therefore, that there is a built-in limitation to opening up the court house doors to citizens whom have had their rights violated. This is another good reason why the courts like the idea of broadening the scope of constitutional civil liability.

Vindication of Rights

There is a silver lining in that officers are being sued for very minor constitutional violations and juries are returning $1.00 verdicts in such cases. Also, often plaintiffs cannot receive compensation for jail time spent based upon unconstitutional seizures.

Martin v Marinez, 934 F3d 594 (2019)
Martin was driving when he was pulled over. Martin said he did not commit a traffic offense, but the officers alleged that Martin's tail and brake lights were not working.

Martin told the officers that his license had been "taken for a ticket." The officers asked Martin to step out of the car. By this time there were at least four officers at the scene. The officers handcuffed Martin, patted him down, and put him in the back seat of a police car. The officers searched the car and found a 9 mm semiautomatic handgun with a defaced serial number and a baggie of cocaine. Later, officers learned that Martin had been convicted of murder and unlawful use of a weapon by a convicted felon.

Martin filed a motion to suppress, and the state dismissed the charges.

Martin filed a Section 1983 suit based primarily on an alleged Fourth Amendment violation contending that:

- his tail and brake lights were working when he was stopped;
- he handed the ticket to the officer as his license had been taken;
- the handgun was under the seat and, therefore, not in open view.

The jury found in favor of Martin on the issue of the constitutionality of the stop. Basically, finding that the tail and brake lights were working.

The district court judge ruled that Martin could not receive recompense for his jail time as a prevailing plaintiff should not be able to collect damages as a result of the "fruit of the poisonous tree" doctrine. So by virtue of that ruling, the jury was unaware of the time Martin spent in jail, as that was irrelevant.

Martin had spent 65 days in jail prior to the suppression hearing. The Seventh Circuit ruled that Martin could not be recompensed for his time in jail. The court reasoned that he had already had the benefit of the exclusionary rule that provided for suppression even though he was guilty. Why should he also have the benefit of money damages for his time in jail when he was guilty?

The courts and the jury found that Martin's "injuries" were limited to the unconstitutional seizure <u>before probable cause existed</u>. As a result, Martin could only receive nominal damages for the officers' stopping Martin without reasonable suspicion (injuries prior to the officers' having probable cause to arrest).

XIII. Other Constitutional Torts

There are a number of constitutional tort issues that have nothing to do with the Fourth, Fifth, or Sixth Amendments. This book deals primarily with constitutional criminal procedure, so most of these constitutional torts are beyond the scope of the book. Classic examples of a constitutional tort falling outside this scope are complaints brought by prisoners under the Eighth Amendment's prohibition against cruel and unusual punishment.

> *There is an enormous body of law in this area; so if you work with prisoners, you must know the law.*

First Amendment Issues

The First Amendment allows persons the right of free speech. The courts have expanded First Amendment rights probably far beyond any possible right dreamed of by the creator(s) of the amendment.

For example, the Seventh Circuit recently held that a person has a First Amendment right to audio tape (and video tape) officers when the officers are performing their official duties in a public place [ACLU v Alvarez, 679 F3d 583 (2012)]. Alvarez, the Cook County State's Attorney appealed to the United States Supreme Court, but the Supreme Court refused to hear the case.

For the most part, First Amendment rights arise within the context of a person smarting off, swearing, or displaying his middle finger to an officer. There is a lot of case law reflecting that this is protected by the First Amendment. Generally words alone, unless they are threatening or fighting words, are protected. For example, there is a difference between a person arguing with an officer about arresting someone and a person who steps in between the officer and arrestee. See e.g. Mims v City of Eugene, 145 Fed Appx. 194 (9th Cir 2005).

Unless an officer is sure that the conduct constitutes obstructing or some other crime, the officer should just let words go, even if the words are critical of police or attempt diversion.

> **HOUSTON V HILL**, 482 US 451 (1987)
> Hill shouted at police trying to distract them when the police were dealing with Hill's friend during a confrontation. He yelled things like, "Why don't you pick on someone your own size?" The police arrested Hill based on an ordinance that made it unlawful to "abuse or interrupt a policeman in the execution of his duty."
>
> Hill was acquitted and sued Houston claiming that his First Amendment rights had been violated.
>
> The United States Supreme Court basically ruled that unless the "words" constituted fighting words or words specifically reflecting disorderly conduct or words inciting a breach of peace, officers may not arrest.
>
> **LEWIS V CITY OF NEW ORLEANS,** 415 US 130 (1974)
> A passenger in a car allegedly yelled angry confrontational obscenities at an officer who had just asked her husband for his license.
>
> She was convicted of an ordinance that made it a crime "for any person wantonly to curse or revile or to use obscene language toward any member of the police while in the actual performance of his duty."
>
> The United States Supreme Court found the ordinance unconstitutional stating, "A properly trained officer may reasonably be expected to exercise a higher degree of restraint than an average private person, and, therefore, be less likely to respond belligerently" to confrontational words.

Reher v Vivo, 656 F3d 772 (2011)
Reher was apparently videotaping kids in a park. The police were called out. Sgt. Marilyn Gabinski talked to a witness who also had been the victim of harassment by Reher, about which Gabinski was aware. Sgt. Gabinski also knew that the victim had filed orders of protection against Reher. When the Sergeant talked to Reher, he said he was just taping nature. Gabinski told Reher that his story was "bullshit." Reher then said that he didn't want to talk to the "f........ bitch," referring to the Sergeant. An officer then arrested Reher for disorderly conduct.

The Seventh Circuit Court of Appeals ruled that calling an officer a name or videotaping in the park is not a crime. Therefore, the arrest was unconstitutional. However, the court ruled that since there was no case right on point, the officer(s) were entitled to qualified immunity.

LOZMAN V CITY OF RIVIERA BEACH, 138 S.Ct. 1945 (2018)
A man, Lozman, spent a lot of time at council meetings criticizing the council, etc. At one meeting a councilman told an officer to arrest Lozman when Lozman wouldn't shut up.

The United States Supreme Court ruled that if there was probable cause, the officer may arrest Lozman. However, Lozman may sue successfully if the council violated his First Amendment rights.

Speaking at public meetings is a very important First Amendment right. Be careful!

COHEN V CALIFORNIA, 403 US 15 (1971)
Cohen walked through a courthouse corridor wearing a jacket that read on the back "F... the Draft." Women and children were present, so the officer arrested Cohen for disturbing the peace.

The United States Supreme Court ruled that this offensive language was protected by the First Amendment and that the arrest was unconstitutional.

Ford v Yakima, 706 F3d 1188 (9th Cir 2014)
An officer stopped Ford's car for a violation that the officer could either cite and release or arrest. The officer was going to just cite and release, but the driver was so abusive in his language that ultimately the officer decided to arrest Ford to teach him a lesson. The officer explained that he was arresting Ford for "running his mouth." He further said that Ford had "diarrhea of the mouth," and that he wouldn't have been arrested if he had kept his mouth shut and cooperated.

The Ninth Circuit ruled that even though there was probable cause to arrest, the arrest was unconstitutional because the officer did not arrest Ford for that crime. He arrested him for exercising his constitutional (First Amendment) rights.

Sharpe v Orange, ___F3d___ (9th Cir 2017)
Merritt Sharpe III was at home when he was arrested on a warrant which should have been executed against Merritt Sharpe IV. After M Sharpe III was handcuffed, he was very angry and used abusive words against the officers. Even after the officers determined that M Sharpe III was the wrong person to arrest, they kept him handcuffed (tightly) because they wanted to teach him a lesson. The police told him that the reason they didn't uncuff Sharpe when they knew he was the wrong arrestee was because of his mouthing off. Later, M Sharpe III sued under section 1983.

The Ninth Circuit ruled that a person who has been unconstitutionally handcuffed must be released as soon as officers determine they have the wrong person. Second, officers cannot continue to handcuff a person to punish him for exercising his First Amendment rights.

Haggerty v Texas Southern University, 391 F3d 653 (2004)
Haggerty, a teacher at Texas Southern University (TSU), saw that about eight students were beating up a student named Randolph. Haggerty called TSU officers. An officer handcuffed Randolph as he was "out of control." Haggerty told the officers not to handcuff Randolph. Officers told Haggerty to back off, or he would be arrested. Shortly thereafter, Randolph apparently tried to break free and attack the students, so the officer slammed Randolph against a wall. Haggerty again attempted to intervene. Walking toward the officer from about 10 to 15 feet away, he told the officer not to "manhandle that juvenile." The officers then arrested Haggerty for interference with the duties of a public servant.

The trial court held that the officer should have known that a person (Haggerty) cannot be arrested when the "interference" consists of "speech only." Therefore, the court denied the motion to grant the officer qualified immunity.

The Fifth Circuit Court of Appeals reversed, ruling that a reasonable officer could have mistakenly believed that there was probable cause to arrest, especially because Haggerty was approaching the officer as he spoke and because the officers had not yet gotten control of the scene. Therefore, the court ruled that qualified immunity was appropriate in this case.

> *Always be careful about arresting someone for talking. Remember the First Amendment guarantees freedom of speech.*

Due Process Violations

Due process basically means fairness. If a court believes that the only conduct the officer is potentially liable for is unfair, the court has to tie that to the constitution.

Benigni v City of Hemet, 879 F2d 473 (1988)
Officers constantly talked to patrons inside and outside a bar. Benigni, the owner, brought a Section 1983 suit against the officers, alleging that officers harassed his patrons in order to drive Benigni out of business. The officers, for example, would enter the bar sometimes as often as six times a night and would go behind the bar, checking drawers, etc.

The jury awarded compensatory damages against the city of $285,000; compensatory damages of $7,500 and punitive damages of $7,500 against the chief; and compensatory damages of $2,500 and punitive damages of $3,000 against the officers involved.

The Ninth Circuit Court of Appeals ruled that neither summary judgment nor qualified immunity were available to the defendants.

Most of the time, these due process issues will arise in the context of a duty an officer had that he/she didn't perform. Normally, it is some duty the officer took on him/herself.

There are numerous cases and situations that hold that an officer sometimes has an affirmative duty to a citizen to act. Most of these cases are ones where the officer created the situation that impacted the citizen to make him/her more vulnerable.

Another circumstance where an officer can be successfully sued for failure to act is when the officer sees another officer violating a citizen's rights and the officer fails to intervene. An officer who is present and fails to intervene to prevent other law enforcement officers from infringing the constitutional rights of citizens is liable under Section 1983 if that officer had reason to know:

- Excessive force was being used. Thompson v Boggs, 33 F3d 847 (1994)
- A citizen has been unjustifiably arrested.
- Any constitutional violation has been committed by a law enforcement official, and the officer had a realistic opportunity to prevent the harm from occurring.
- The officer promises protection in a situation, but fails to provide it. (See Kennedy v Ridgefield, below.)

Byrd v Brishke, 466 F2d 6 (1972)
Officers arrested a felon, Byrd, who was later convicted and given five years in prison.

The officers allegedly beat Byrd with fists, feet, nightsticks, etc. They then threw him into a police car so that his face hit the floor.

Officers who saw this but failed to intervene were denied qualified immunity.

Regalado v Chicago, 40 F Supp 2d 1009 (ND IL 1999)
Officers had an arrest warrant for Regalado. When the officers saw Regalado, he ran. When the officers caught him, they handcuffed him and continued to hit him with their flashlights, etc. Some officers apparently looked on while the officers beat Regalado. Witnesses saw this. Regalado was seriously injured.

Regalado's guardian sued.

The Seventh Circuit Court of Appeals ruled that whether the officer was not intervening when another officer was using excessive force was a question for the jury. Qualified immunity could not be granted.

Abdullahi v Madison, 423 F3d 763 (2005)
Jamal Mohamed (hereafter victim) was acting crazy. He slugged a nurse who tried to help him and then started to swing his belt around. Officers arrived and had much difficulty subduing the victim. After the victim was on his stomach, an officer put all his weight on the victim's back. It was agreed that the officer's knee was in the victim's back for about 30 seconds. Medical testimony revealed that the victim died from chest and neck trauma consistent with the crushing of the victim's chest.

The victim's administrator brought this suit under Section 1983, alleging that the officer kept his full weight on the victim after the victim was handcuffed, and that the other officers did nothing to get the officer off of the victim after he was subdued on his stomach.

The Seventh Circuit Court of Appeals ruled that the officers involved were not entitled to qualified immunity, as there was a material issue of fact as to whether excessive force was administered and whether the other officers should have intervened and told the officer to get off the victim. Therefore, the case was remanded for a jury trial.

Riordan v Joliet, 3 F Supp 2d 889 (No IL 1998)
Riordan, a drunk, was staying at the Sports Center, sort of a YMCA. He got very drunk one night and made a pest of himself, so police were called. The police took Riordan to the station in his bare feet and no coat, since Riordan wouldn't put a coat or shoes on.

The officers dropped Riordan off at the lobby of the police station and told him to stay there all night. Riordan wandered off in below 20° weather and fell asleep. Riordan lost his toes and got very sick.

The Seventh Circuit Court of Appeals ruled that the officers were not entitled to summary judgment. Once the officers took custody of Riordan, they were responsible for his safety.

Kennedy v Ridgefield, 440 F3d 1091 (2006)
An officer took a report from a victim's mother, Kennedy, alleging that the neighbor boy was molesting her daughter. Kennedy asked the officer to notify her if the officer contacted the suspect. She was concerned as there had been rumors that the suspect had issued death threats previously. Kennedy contacted the police several times during the next two weeks inquiring about the investigation and reminding the officers about the necessity of contacting her before contacting the suspect.

An officer contacted and interrogated the suspect without notifying Kennedy first. The officer then went next door and told Kennedy that he had contacted the suspect. Kennedy then became frightened that the suspect would retaliate. The officer assured the victim that the police would patrol the area.

That night the suspect broke into the victim's home and shot and killed the woman's husband.

Kennedy sued the police under Section 1983.

The Ninth Circuit Court of Appeals ruled that the officers could not afford themselves of qualified immunity as they had knowingly given assurances to the plaintiff and then did not protect her and her family.

> *Never tell a woman that an order of protection will protect her from her spouse, boyfriend, etc. And do not say that you will respond immediately if she calls.*

Wood v Ostander, 879 F2d 583 (1989)
Officers arrested the driver of a car in a bad neighborhood and impounded the car. A female passenger was told to find her own way home. She was raped.

The Ninth Circuit Court of Appeals ruled that the officers may be liable.

Munger v Glasgow, PD, 227 F3d 1082 (2000)
Officers responded to a problem drunk in a bar. The officers removed the drunk, Munger, from the bar. It was very cold out and Munger only had a t-shirt on. The officers told Munger not to drive his truck, so Munger wandered off. The next day he was found a couple of blocks away, dead.

The Ninth Circuit ruled that the officers had put Munger in danger through some affirmative conduct. Therefore, the officers were denied qualified immunity.

Penilla v City of Huntington Park, 115 F3d 707 (1997)
Penilla became seriously ill while sitting on his porch. Officers arrived and found Penilla to be in serious need of medical services. The officers then broke into Penilla's home and deposited Penilla there. The next day Penilla's family members found Penilla dead.

Penilla's estate sued for Fourth and Fourteenth Amendment violations. The defendant/officers moved to dismiss based on qualified immunity. The district court ruled that there was case law supporting the proposition that the officers had an affirmative duty to Penilla once they had begun the process and that there was no theory for entering Penilla's home.

The Ninth Circuit affirmed, ruling that the "officers in this case allegedly took affirmative actions that significantly increased the risk facing Penilla" and that there are lots of cases that stand for the proposition that if an officer exposes a person to danger, they are liable for the consequences. Therefore, qualified immunity was not appropriate, and the case was remanded for a jury trial—and the fairly certain awarding of compensatory and punitive damages.

Gibson v County of Washoe, 290 F3d 1175 (2002)
Gibson was a manic-depressive. He was going through a manic phase where he was acting weirdly at a convenience store. His wife reported that he had a loaded weapon with him and that he had just threatened to kill his wife. After Gibson was subdued, they took him to the jail. Officers found the pills to control his mental illness in Gibson's truck, and they gave them to the nurse in charge at the jail. Gibson acted violent, so the officers restrained him more and more and sprayed him with pepper spray. Gibson then had a heart attack and died.

The Ninth Circuit court of Appeals ruled that the officers who brought Gibson in had an affirmative duty to try to convey his medicine to responsible personnel, which they did. Therefore, they could not be held liable for Gibson's death, but the nurse could and so could the department.

Estate of Burton Walter Amos v City of Page, 257 F3d 1086 (2001)
Amos was in a car accident near a wilderness area. Amos got out of the car and stumbled away. Officers who arrived at the scene told private rescuers to go home. The officers then tried to find Amos, but their flashlights lost power. A helicopter cut off the search fearing nearby power lines. No one continued the search until over a month later. Three years later Amos' body was discovered nearby.

The Ninth Circuit ruled that the officers did not create the danger here. Therefore, there was no constitutional violation.

> *The court distinguished a case where officers stopped a private search for a boy in the water who had just gone under. The officers waited for government rescuers, who were way too late to save the boy.*

Florek v Mundelein, 649 F3d 594 (2011)
Officers executed a search warrant. The resident complained of having a heart attack. The officers apparently refused to give her a baby aspirin and/or call an ambulance.

The Seventh Circuit Court of Appeals ruled that the officers deserved qualified immunity on the aspirin claim. And the claim of refusal to call an ambulance went to a jury and the jury resolved the case in favor of the defendant(s) as the officers were unaware that Florek was experiencing a heart attack. As soon as it was apparent that Florek was experiencing a heart attack, an ambulance was called.

> *If the medical need is apparent and serious, an officer must attend to it—or be liable.*

XIII. Costs and Reputations

There are a number of reasons why Section 1983 actions have become so important to officers.

- Everyone has a video camera now, and everything officers do in public is captured on video. Many times, the video is much worse than what actually occurred.
- Certain physical contacts, such as dealing with the mentally ill, are judged under the GRAHAM standard, which assumes officers are dealing with a criminal.

- In general, trials have become extremely expensive, so most cases are settled, even if the officers did nothing wrong or their constitutional violations were not serious.

Crosby v Evanston (Settled)
A woman called 911 saying that she could see an "African-American" man breaking into a car. Officers stopped the car, and the African-American, Crosby, got out of the car and put his hands in the air apparently even before he was told to. Many officers were at the scene yelling instructions to Crosby. Crosby continued to stand there, not moving, with his hands high in the air. The officers took Crosby to the ground and handcuffed him. Crosby asked what he was being arrested for. An officer said to Crosby that they had a report that he (Crosby) had stolen the car. Crosby said he was a doctoral engineering student at Northwestern and had bought the car. He then gave details about the fact that he was the owner.

The case was settled just prior to trial for $1,250,000.

Fox v Hayes, 600 F3d 819 (7th Cir 2010)
Fox called police because his daughter was missing. She was found soon thereafter in a nearby creek bound, sexually assaulted, and murdered.

Officers asked Fox to come to the station. He did. After he was there and officers accused Fox of murdering his daughter, Fox yelled that he would never do that and tried to leave. The officer said, "Sit your ass down." Fox did so. (This was probably when the jury felt custody/arrest began.) Officers suggested that Fox take a polygraph, and he apparently failed it. Officers then interrogated Fox for several hours and obtained a confession.

Eight months later, the DNA from the sperm was examined and determined not to have come from Fox. The state's attorney dismissed the case, and Fox sued under Section 1983.

The state argued that there was probable cause for the arrest for the following undisputed reasons:

- Fox looked for his daughter for 40 minutes before calling police.
- Fox did not call his wife immediately upon determining that the daughter was gone.
- Fox did not reveal that he watched an adult video the night of the murder.
- A vehicle that looked like Fox's was seen at a nearby gas station during the time Fox said he was home. (However, the license number of the vehicle could not be seen.)

Both the jury and the Seventh Circuit Court of Appeals ruled that these facts reflected that Fox was in custody and the facts did not rise to the level of probable cause. The jury awarded Fox $15,500,000. The Seventh Circuit affirmed the verdict (but reduced the award).

GLOSSARY

ABANDONMENT
Persons abandon property when they throw it away, leave it behind, or deny possession or ownership of it. When suspects abandon property, they normally lose their reasonable expectation of privacy in the property and their standing to object to admission of the property in court.

ADMINISTRATIVE SEARCH
An administrative search is an exception to the warrant requirement. Courts condone such searches (because they are minor intrusions) when they are conducted for a very important governmental purpose which is non-crime related. Some administrative searches can be conducted only with an administrative warrant.

ADMINISTRATIVE WARRANT
An administrative warrant permits very limited intrusions (searches and/or seizures) on less than probable cause when the public interest (importance) is great and there is no reasonable alternative.

AFFIANT
An affiant is a person (usually an officer) who swears under oath to the truth of an affidavit.

AFFIDAVIT
An affidavit is a sworn statement supporting a warrant to search or arrest.

ANONYMOUS INFORMANT
An anonymous informant is a person who gives officers crime-related information but does not tell officers who he/she is. An anonymous informant can create reasonable suspicion or even probable cause depending upon how much crime-related corroboration officers can find by investigation.

ARREST
For purposes of this book, an arrest is the same for Fourth or Fifth Amendment purposes. That is, arrest for Fourth Amendment purposes is the same as "restraint in a significant way" for determining custody prior to giving Miranda warnings for Fifth Amendment purposes.

AUTOMOBILE EXCEPTION
Officers may normally search vehicles if they possess probable cause.

BAD ACT
A bad act is any "bad" conduct by the defendant other than the crime with which he/she is charged. These bad acts are normally not admissible.

BURDEN OF PROOF
The burden of proof is the responsibility of one party (1) to go forward with evidence, and (2) ultimately to prove the proposition. Some propositions (e.g. the voluntariness of consent) must be proven by a preponderance of the evidence (which is more than likely). Some propositions (like the constitutionality of an arrest) must be proven by a probability (less than preponderance), and convictions must be proven beyond a reasonable doubt.

CAUSE OF ACTION
A cause of action is a valid legal basis which the courts recognize for the filing of a civil suit.

CLOSED CONTAINER
A closed container is an object capable of holding other objects (and the officer cannot see inside the enclosing object without opening it). A closed container may be searched only with a valid search theory.

CONFIDENTIAL INFORMANT
A confidential informant is a person who is known by the state (officers) and who gives officers crime-related information. This informant does not want to have his/her identity disclosed to the defense.

CONSENT
Consent is one of the major theories permitting officers to enter areas where a suspect has a reasonable expectation of privacy.

CONTACT
A contact is a discussion between officers and suspects where there is no control of the suspects by the officers; i.e., a reasonable person in the suspect's position would feel free to walk away or ignore the officer.

CORROBORATION
Corroboration is information supporting information obtained from other sources (usually informants) that tends to prove that there is evidence in a certain place or that a person is committing or has committed a crime.

CRIME-RELATED EVIDENCE
Crime-related evidence is any property, statement, or identification that the state gathers to use against a suspect in court. This is evidence which ties a suspect to a crime in any way.

CURTILAGE
The area around premises that is protected by the Fourth Amendment.

CUSTODY
Custody is the same as arrest or restraint in a significant way. It is unconstitutional to take a suspect into custody without probable cause for Fourth Amendment purposes. Officers must warn suspects in custody before taking a statement for Fifth Amendment purposes.

DETENTION
Detention is the period of time after a lawful stop based on reasonable suspicion when officers may freeze a suspect while investigating the crime to determine whether there is probable cause. During this period, officers may ask the suspect questions without warning him/her, bring witnesses in to identify the suspect, search (frisk) the suspect if the officers reasonably fear for their safety, and conduct other basic investigation for a brief period of time. Stop and detention are often used synonymously because they require the same level of suspicion and it is difficult often to know when one stops and the other begins.

DICTUM
Dictum is information in a case that is not precedential. It is often interesting opinions, etc., by judges—but often it is BS.

DISCLOSURE/DISCOVERY
The state must disclose to the defense all evidence it intends to introduce at trial including reports, statements, etc. Officers must ensure that prosecutors are aware of all evidence, as it may not be introduced at trial unless the defense attorney is made aware of it relatively early in the process. If the defense learns of information that should have been disclosed—but wasn't—the case may be dismissed.

DOCTRINE
A doctrine is a body of law that directly relates circumstance or legal principle. This term is often used interchangeably with the term theory.

EMERGENCY
An emergency is normally a life, injury, or illness-threatening circumstance, which permits officers to search or seize without a warrant or even probable cause or any other theory. Illinois courts generally rule that the emergency doctrine is a subset of the exigency doctrine.

EXCLUSIONARY RULE
The exclusionary rule is the rule which provides for the suppression of evidence that is gathered in violation of a defendant's rights. The evidence must be thrown out in order to deter officers from violating citizens' rights.

EXIGENCY
An exigency is a circumstance that calls for an immediate response from officers. Exigencies morph depending on the circumstances. An exigency relating to the search of a home is different from the exigency related to a vehicle or closed container. Usually the term implies that officers have probable cause, but they are unable to get a warrant. Therefore, the officers may search or seize without the warrant.

FEDERALISM
Federalism is the federal-state relationship that separates federal constitutional doctrine from state constitutional doctrine. The United States Supreme Court, of course, sets minimum constitutional standards for officers. However, state courts may set higher standards for police which also give "more rights" to the citizens of the particular state.

FRISK
A frisk or patdown is also called a search incident to detention in this book. This search is permissible when an officer has seized a suspect on reasonable suspicion and further reasonably suspects that the detainee has access to a weapon.

FRUIT OF THE POISONOUS TREE
Crime-related evidence gathered eventually as the result of an earlier violation is also inadmissible in court.

GOOD FAITH EXCEPTION TO THE EXCLUSIONARY RULE
The good faith doctrine permits the introduction of evidence, even if officers violate a suspect's rights in the gathering of evidence. Good faith usually means the officers' reliance on a warrant, reliance on a statute or ordinance, or reliance on case law. Under Illinois statute "good faith means whenever a peace officer obtains evidence... pursuant to a search or an arrest warrant obtained from a neutral and detached judge, which warrant is free from obvious defects other than non-deliberate errors in preparation and contains no material misrepresentations by any agent of the State, and the officer reasonably believed the warrant to be valid" [Ill.Rev.Stat.1987, Ch. 38, par. 114-12(b) (2)].

HEARSAY
Hearsay is a statement made by someone who didn't actually see, smell, feel, etc., whatever the information is about. The person talking is simply repeating what someone else told them. That's why hearsay generally is not admissible at trial unless it fits an exception that gives the statement an air of truthfulness, like a confession (because who would confess unless the statement is true?). Hearsay is also permissible for purposes of getting a warrant and admissible during many pretrial hearings.

IMPEACHMENT
Impeachment occurs when an attorney cross examines a witness and shows him to be lying, mistaken, prejudiced, etc. Officers are most commonly impeached by their own reports or the reports of other officers.

IMPOUNDMENT
Impoundment is the seizing of a vehicle or house or other property for lawful purposes.

INTERROGATION
Interrogation for purposes of Miranda is any question or statement that might elicit a response. Under the Fifth Amendment, there is no difference between an interview and an interrogation.

INVENTORY
An inventory is usually related to the search of a vehicle, which comes into officers' hands lawfully. An inventory is conducted to protect the owners' property and to protect the officers from false claims of theft. An Inventory sheet must also be left after the seizure of property after the execution of a search warrant.

MIRANDA WARNING
Miranda warnings must be given to all suspects in custody prior to interrogation. These warnings reflect the explanation of the suspect's Fifth Amendment rights to remain silent and have his attorney present prior to any questioning.

NEGLIGENCE
Negligence is doing of an act or failure to do an act which a reasonable officer would do, and the act or the failure to act causes injury or damages.

OPEN FIELD
An open field is an area outside the curtilage where a person does not have a reasonable expectation of privacy. Therefore, officers may enter these areas without a warrant, probable cause, or even reasonable suspicion.

OPEN VIEW
Open view is the officers' viewing of crime-related evidence within an area where a suspect has a high expectation of privacy while standing outside that area. Therefore, although the officer can see the evidence, they may not seize it. The most classic illustration of this situation is when officers can lawfully see through the window of a home and view crime-related evidence.

PEN REGISTER
A pen register is a device that records the phone numbers called by a suspect.

PER SE TEST
A per se test compares the conduct of officers to particular rules that must be followed with very few exceptions. Miranda is such a test in that Fifth Amendment warnings are absolutely (almost always) required before questioning a suspect in custody. This is opposed to the totality of circumstances test that simply allows all factors to be considered in the determination of the constitutional propriety of the officers' conduct.

PLAIN VIEW
Plain view searches and seizures occur when an officer is lawfully present where they see crime-related evidence. Plain view is almost always a scope issue. That is, assuming the entry of the private area was constitutional, did the officers stay within the appropriate scope of their original theory for entry?

PREMISES
Premises include homes, businesses, structures, and areas surrounding whether protected by the Fourth Amendment or not.

PROBABLE CAUSE
The amount of evidence—more than reasonable suspicion but less than a preponderance—necessary to obtain a warrant to search or arrest. Probable cause in addition to exigency also permits an officer to search or seize.

PROTECTIVE SWEEP
A protective sweep is a search of a home after a lawful arrest in order to ensure that no other suspects who could attack the officers are in the home. There must be reasonable suspicion to believe that such a person exists before such searches are constitutional.

QUALIFIED IMMUNITY
An officer can claim qualified immunity from a Section 1983 law suit if the law in the area related to the alleged constitutional violation has not been firmly established even if in this case the court rules the officer violated the plaintiff's constitutional rights.

REASONABLE EXPECTATION OF PRIVACY
The courts determine the areas of citizens' lives where they can reasonably expect privacy. When officers enter these areas, they must be "armed with" a search theory permitting the entry, because such intrusions are "searches" protected by the Fourth Amendment.

REASONABLE SUSPICION
Reasonable suspicion is an amount of evidence more than a hunch but less than probable cause. Stops and frisks are permitted only if the officer possesses reasonable suspicion at the time of the stop and frisk.

RELIABILITY OF IDENTIFICATION
Witnesses may testify about a prior identification and identify a defendant in court, even if the prior identification was unconstitutionally suggestive, if the prior identification was reliable. If the basis of the witnesses' identification was the independent basis of the original crime, the identification is reliable.

RELIABILITY OF INFORMANT
Reliability when applied to an informant usually relates to whether the informant is a citizen or a paid informant. Citizen informants are normally automatically reliable, while paid or underworld informants must be made reliable or corroborated.

SCALIA DOCTRINE
Officers may search incident to arrest if there might be evidence related to the arrest in the vehicle.

SEARCH
A search is an "intrusion" by the state (usually officers) into areas where a suspect has a reasonable expectation of privacy. Searches almost always relate to things (while seizures almost always relate to persons).

SEARCH INCIDENT TO DETENTION
A search incident to detention is a search based on fear that a suspect detained on reasonable suspicion may be able to obtain a weapon. These searches are also characterized as TERRY searches. These searches have been extended beyond frisks or patdowns, in that officers may search vehicles or other areas if there is reasonable suspicion to believe that a weapon is within lunging distance.

SEARCH INCIDENT TO ARREST
A search incident to arrest is the search of areas within the immediate control of an arrestee at the time of the arrest. Officers may not search vehicles after the arrestee has been handcuffed, unless there is evidence related to the arrest in the vehicle. Also, the courts may allow the search of the vehicle if there are uncuffed occupants of the vehicle who remain within lunging distance of the vehicle.

SEIZURE
A seizure usually relates to persons. A seizure at its lowest level is a restraint where the detainee is not free to leave. This seizure must be justified by reasonable suspicion. A seizure at its highest constitutional level is an arrest or custody, which can only be justified by probable cause.

STANDING
Standing occurs when a defendant has a reasonable expectation of privacy in the area searched or when the issue relates directly to defendant's personal rights.

STOP
A stop is a seizure which can be justified only by reasonable suspicion. A stop occurs for constitutional purposes when a suspect is not free to leave or ignore the officer.

SUGGESTIVITY
Suggestivity usually relates to identifications. If an identification is unduly suggestive, the court must then determine whether the identification is reliable.

SUMMARY JUDGMENT
Officers who are sued under Section 1983 can seek summary judgment and be removed from the case early. Summary judgment means that, even if the officers concede the facts alleged by the plaintiff(s), the law says that the officers are not liable.

TORT
A tort is a breach of a duty of care that causes damage or injury.

TOTALITY OF CIRCUMSTANCES TEST
The totality of circumstances test is applied by the courts to determine the propriety of officer's conduct. It is, for instance, the test used to determine whether there was probable cause and whether a statement or a consent was voluntarily given. This test is applied in certain circumstances as opposed to the per se test like Miranda.

VEHICLE
A vehicle is a mobile instrument that carries persons and/or things from one place to another.

VOLUNTARINESS OF CONSENT
Voluntariness is the standard used by the courts to determine the admissibility of a consent to search or seize. It is a totality of circumstances test that weighs the good and bad factors in order to determine whether the consent was the product of improperly coercive influences. The state must prove voluntariness by a preponderance of evidence.

VOLUNTARINESS OF STATEMENT
Any time a statement is taken from a suspect, the court must determine that it is voluntary before allowing a jury to hear it. In order to be voluntary, a statement must not be the product of coercion or promises. The courts use a "totality of circumstances" test to decide whether the statement is voluntary.

VOLUNTEERED STATEMENT
A volunteered statement is a statement given by a suspect that is not in response to police interrogation. This statement is admissible, even though the suspect is in custody and has not been warned or if he/she has been warned and has asserted his/her rights.

WARRANT
A court order signed by a judge which permits and/or requires officers to search or seize.

CASE INDEX

SUBJECT INDEX